HEIRS
TOGETHER

ALSO BY PATRICIA GUNDRY . . .
Woman Be Free

HEIRS TOGETHER

PATRICIA GUNDRY

Zondervan Publishing House
Grand Rapids, Michigan

Book Title: HEIRS TOGETHER

Note
Occasionally third person pronouns have been used in ways contrary to strictly proper usage. A book written to men and women as individuals and also as couples has unique pronoun problems. The bending of the rules was to help avoid stilted and awkward usage.

All scripture quotations, unless otherwise noted, are taken from the HOLY BIBLE: NEW INTERNATIONAL VERSION (North American Edition). Copyright © 1978 by The International Bible Society. Used by permission of Zondervan Bible Publishers.

Poems by Susan Polis Schutz from *I Want to Laugh, I Want to Cry,* copyright © 1973 by Continental Publications, are reprinted with permission. All rights reserved.

Poem "For Every Woman" by Nancy R. Smith is used by permission of the publisher.

HEIRS TOGETHER
© 1980 by The Zondervan Corporation
Grand Rapids, Michigan

Zondervan Publishing House,
1415 Lake Drive, S.E.,
Grand Rapids, Michigan 49506

Library of Congress Cataloging in Publicaton Data
Gundry, Patricia.
    Heirs together.

    1. Marriage.   2. Marriage—Biblical teaching.   I. Title.
BV835.G86   248.4   79-25500
ISBN 0-310-25371-3

Printed in the United States of America

85   86   87   88   89   90   91   92 / 15   14   1312   11   10 9 8 7 6 5

Love needs new leaves every summer of life, as much as your elm tree, and new branches to grow broader and wider, and new flowers to cover the ground.

Harriet Beecher Stowe

Contents

HEIRS
HEIRS
HEIRS
HEIRS
HEIRS
TOGETHER

1

1

Kaleidoscope

ka lei do scope (kə lī′də skōp′) *n.* [Gr. *kalos,* beautiful +
eidos, form + SCOPE] 1. a tubelike instrument containing
loose bits of colored glass, plastic, etc. reflected by mir-
rors so that various symmetrical patterns appear when
the tube is held to the eye and rotated. 2. anything that
constantly changes, as in color and pattern.

*Webster's New World Dictionary
of the American Language*

A good marriage is like a kaleidoscope. With a few simple
ingredients it is ever-changing, showing new facets of each
other and the pleasure of working and living and loving as a
team.

A marriage can be whatever you want it to be. It can be as
unique as the combination of two unique people makes it.
Marriage does not have to stay the same; it can become better
and better. It can change as a husband and wife learn and grow
and change.

Your marriage is your very own; it belongs to no one else.
And others have no right to tell you what your marriage should

be like. If you try to live out someone else's idea of marriage, you may be fortunate and stumble onto a pattern that you happen to fit into pretty well. On the other hand, you may get a pattern that does not fit at all. So it is important to realize that it is your marriage and that you can write your own rules (I hope they will really be principles rather than rules). Marriage can be what you make it—together.

When individuals come to marriage, each comes with a mental data bank full of prerecorded information about what marriage should be like. This data has been absorbed unconsciously from every marriage that has been seen or heard about. The mind forms a composite of "What Marriage Should Be Like" or "What Marriage IS Like." Thus, each individual in the marriage has his or her own data bank filled with different information. And that's the rub. Each proceeds to live out his or her own idea of marriage, and often they don't match!

It all seems so simple at first. "If he loved me, he wouldn't mind doing it my way," she thinks. And of course he thinks the same about her. When the clashes flash brightly and loudly, each begins to doubt that the other does love as much as they thought before the marriage. They do not realize that it is not the love or lack of it that is the problem; it is the two different ideas of marriage that are at war.

There are three ways of resolving this aside from kissing each other good-by. One way is to battle it out: win what you can and give in when you have to. This creates the all-too-common "battleground family" or "game-playing family," complete with maneuvers and power plays. Another method is to withdraw from each other, be hurt, and wait for the cold war to warm up on its own—not too pleasant either. The third way is to scrap preconceived notions of what marriage is supposed to be and, step by step, work out the kind of marriage the two of you would like if you could have it any way you want. Most couples use a combination of the first two methods with occasional journeys into the third. But most couples expend little effort, seldom even talking about what they want their marriage to be. They don't seem to realize they can.

I understand why many young couples today talk of living together because they are afraid marriage will destroy their love and compatibility. They have seen so many bad marriages, marriages in which both partners are unhappy, marriages in which destructive games and power struggles are constant ingredients. They do not realize they can choose their manner of married life just as they can choose their manner of living together. Being married is not becoming different people. It is not giving up one's self and one's freedom and individuality. Not unless couples let it be that by following the patterns of other marriages they have seen.

You are rational adults, and you are competent to decide how you want to live as a team. Don't let anyone else, me included, dictate what your marriage should be. Of course, you can use information from other sources. Why should you have to make all the mistakes yourself? You can profit from the insights of others. But don't assume anyone knows more about the two of you and how you should relate and live than the two of you know.

If you are believers, and I am assuming you are because this is a biblically oriented book, you will want to use biblical principles in working out your marriage and deciding what it will be. But be careful in deciding which principles really are biblical. Just because someone who writes a book or has some kind of following or credentials says it is biblical does not guarantee that it is. Most people are mistaken at least some of the time, even sincere, godly people. Read the Bible for yourself. Talk about it. Pray about it. Go as God leads you.

If you decide you want a marriage of equal persons, that this is a kind of marriage that appeals to you and that you feel is based upon biblical principles and attitudes toward each other, you will probably find you will need to make several changes in the way you live in your marriage. This may involve an extensive overhaul or it may only be a matter of clarifying values you already have but have never applied directly to your marriage.

Part of the problem with marriages today is that we set

such high expectations for marriage in our society. We are unrealistic about what marriage can do. We load marriages too heavily, and when they fall, we feel the institution itself is to blame. In many other cultures not nearly so much is expected of marriage. Also, their marriages are not based upon love unions and shared intimacy. They are arranged by others, usually parents, thought to be wiser than the participants. Partners are selected for temperamental compatibility, financial security, and other practical reasons.

In our culture, we say we marry for love. And when we have difficulties, we of course assume that the love wasn't what it should have been or that it has sickened and died. Those people from across the world would laugh at us. They know that marriage is work and commitment. And if love comes, if they grow to love the one they marry, that is a bonus for their efforts. We cannot imagine ourselves marrying first and loving later. And yet we are willing to toss out the marriage when we feel love has been inadequate. We do not believe we can make it grow again, or grow better than before. To us, a marriage is either perfect or useless, a conclusion we would immediately recognize as unreasonable and unrealistic in any other area.

Marriage *is* work. Some fortunate few couples are so suited to each other that they seem to glide effortlessly along without conflict or doubt. But they are rare. Most of us must work at our marriages constantly to build up broken places, remodel the rooms, sand off the rough spots, and plump up the cushions. When you think of it, it is really amazing that we treat the most important alliance in our lives as though it must maintain itself without our wholehearted effort. No wonder that is called a *romantic* view. (The dictionary definition of romantic is "unrealistic.")

The problem in marriage is not the love. The problem is that love cannot carry the burden alone. Love is the oil that makes the machinery of marriage run smoothly and hum with satisfaction. But we must tend the machine. We must repair, and adjust, and maintain it. Love cannot do it all.

And love *can* grow. Live in loving ways, says the Book of Ephesians. Love as brothers, as dearly loved children. We can feed love. We can welcome it and make a comfortable place for it. And we can ask God to help us love where it has shrunk or faded. We can ask Him to show us how to encourage love in another.

And that is what a marriage of equals is based upon. Love. I love you enough to let you be the real you. And you love me enough to let me be the real me. And let's do it together, love.

TOGETHER

2

2

What's Wrong?

"I now pronounce you person and person," read the cartoon caption. My first thought was—what a witty commentary on the kind of contemporary marriage that is so open as to be almost empty!

I put the magazine down and went about my work. Then another thought came to me . . . *to still be whole persons after marriage . . . to be affirmed as individuals by marriage instead of having your individuality stamped out or stamped upon. How fine it would be to expand marriage to fit the people instead of shrinking the people to fit an institution.* And I realized I had identified a central problem couples face today in marriage.

Many people now feel marriage demands that they give up their own personalities and dreams. They fear it will destroy the very uniqueness each brought to the union and, eventually, bring on an oppressive stagnation. They fear marriage will even destroy their love.

Don't ever say wife to me
it's too cold
if someone asks who I am
tell them I am the one you love
if they quiver, "Are you married?"
then say that we are sharing our lives together.[1]

What has happened to make so many feel this way? Is there something wrong with them? Something wrong with marriage? But hasn't marriage always been the same? And wasn't it more satisfying than this to our ancestors? If it is not satisfying now, why not?

I think we can find reasons for our widespread dissatisfaction with marriage now. And knowing the reasons, we can look for solutions to our dissatisfactions in a more reasonable manner than we have been doing. We will be looking at marriage itself to find out what its true essence is. We will be boiling it all down to its basic ingredient as a beginning point in our search for ways to make marriage better and more satisfying here and now.

Christians are in a double bind. While they experience the same pressures other married people are dealing with now, they must carry an extra load that is theirs alone: Christians feel their marriages should always work well just because they *are* Christians. They think because they prayed for God's guidance in choosing a partner He will not allow them to be really unhappy in their marriage. So when unhappiness comes, they are disillusioned and feel cheated. They wonder if they did choose the person who was "God's will" for them. And if they didn't, what do they do now? If their love was real in the beginning, why doesn't it bridge the gap between them? It is a lonely, painful dilemma.

Too many books on marriage written by and for Christians give formulas and rules guaranteeing success if those formulas and rules are followed. These books instruct wives to obey, husbands to lead, and each to love, implying or even promising that all will then work out miraculously. When it doesn't, the unhappy partners sink deeper into their disappointment and think there is something dreadfully wrong with them. Or, they become embittered at "Christian" advice with its impracticalities and pat answers and drift away from the church.

Is there such a thing as *Christian* marriage? Do Christians have some corner on the truth that makes them more able to have good marriages than the world-at-large? Most of us know non-Christian couples who are happy and content with each other, and fervent Christians who betray the hidden strain of a marriage that is not so good. I say betray because most Christians feel they must cover up an unhappy marriage. It isn't *nice* for Christians to have difficult marriages. It is a shameful secret. They must hide the damning evidence.

It is as though we cannot accept the reality of serious problems within Christians' marriages. In fact, our attitude toward divorced Christians reflects our unwillingness to admit to ourselves the truth about marriage problems among us.

Let's face it. Christians do have difficulties in marriage. We need to stop ignoring the problem. We need to examine the pat answers and formulas so widely accepted for so long in Christian circles to see if they are biblical at all. Advice like the following illustrates the kind of simplistic and useless help Christians are receiving.

> How do you overcome the fear of your husband driving too fast? Recognize that God is in control and whatever happens is within His will. . . . Remember also the "Father-filtered" principle and, as Mary might suggest, "Pray for a policeman."[2]

If all advice was merely ridiculous, the situation would be bad enough. But some advice has had tragic results.

> In 1971, *Fascinating Womanhood* took our church by storm. Some of us women had been meeting in small groups and had confessed to discontent in our marriages. Here, said one eager advocate, was the answer to our problem. We all bought copies and began meeting for discussions.
> Our fellowship had begun as a Bible study for Christians searching for a New Testament faith. After FW, it was only natural that we began to take all the scriptures

regarding women in the most literal sense. Some of the women began wearing head-covers to indicate their submissiveness. We were instructed to deliberately stifle the gifts of the Holy Spirit which we had always practiced in church, so that our husbands would be forced to take a more active role. It was constantly emphasized how important the leadership of men was—since Eve had been deceived, our sex was forever unfit for any kind of decision-making or administration.

Here and there you would hear of a woman having a time with her "rebellion." For instance, a friend of mine had a very difficult childbirth with complications. This, she was told, was God's punishment for having been unsubmissive. When her husband recommended she have a tubal ligation, she felt she dare not disagree. Though tears streamed down her face all the way to the hospital, the operation was performed. Later, she fell into a deep depression and lost all sexual feelings. When she spoke to the pastor about these problems, he advised her to fake it.[3]

A growing number of believers are questioning these old formulas and roles taught for so long as the only biblical way to relate in marriage. They are measuring the claims behind those formulas and role expectations against sound Bible interpretation. Finding the roles and formulas inadequate, they are moving on into a relationship of equals based on firmer biblical footing.

My husband and I are among them. Years ago we tried to pattern our marriage according to the rules we had been taught. He tried to lead and I tried to follow. We worked to squeeze ourselves into the narrow confines we had been told was our place. We didn't fit very well, but we thought it was just us, so we kept trying. Over the years through our own personal Bible study, we gradually came to doubt that the basis for those traditional teachings was biblical. We became convinced the Bible does not give us rigid rules for marriage or roles we must copy. Instead, we found biblical *principles* applicable to all relationships, including marriage. And the overriding principle for relationships among believers seemed to be that of mutual submission.

A marriage based on the principle of mutual submission

goes beyond roles and formulas and makes them unnecessary. It becomes a marriage of equal persons and makes possible the intimacy so many people are longing for today.

I suppose these questions immediately come to mind after reading what I have just said: "If the traditional teachings about marriage are not biblical, why have so many good and sincere Bible teachers been convinced they were?" And, "Isn't the Bible absolutely clear on the subject?"

My answer to the second question is: "Not if you do not have all the data you need to interpret the Bible." "Not if you are prejudiced, however unintentionally, by a tradition based on doctrine you reject." The answer to the first is: We have a long history in the church of relying too strongly on tradition without enough careful study of the biblical evidence. Let me explain further.

Traditional teachings about marriage are not as firmly founded on the Bible as many would believe. Actually, they are based on medieval theology. (We will examine that theology and trace the traditional views on marriage in chapter 4.) Later, the Reformers rejected much of the medieval dogma, but did not always eliminate longstanding practices based upon it. Marriage laws in pre-Christian Celtic Britain gave men and women equal rights in marriage and divorce. After the medieval church gained power in Britain, laws were changed to harmonize with its view of men, women, and marriage. Practices soon reflected this new stance. Later, the origin of those discriminatory laws and practices was easily overlooked, and they were left to stand.

By canon law a husband was entitled to beat his wife. Canon law allowed only the dowry system for matrimony, and under this system women were defenseless. Moreover, since they were legally incompetent, they were not considered fit to give testimony in court. In general, they were considered as man's property, women were pawns in the game of acquiring wealth. The Church's complicated marriage laws offered ample opportunity for trickery and abuse.[4]

Although we do not realize it, our modern teaching still reflects the medieval church's beliefs about marriage. We have based much of our advice to husbands and wives on rules and attitudes originated by a celibate religious hierarchy who believed sex was sinful and women inferior, even evil.

Thomas Aquinas, the father of medieval theology, said: As regards the individual nature, woman is defective and misbegotten, for the active force in the male seed tends to the production of a perfect likeness in the masculine sex; while the production of women comes from a defect in the active force or from some material indisposition, or even from some external influence, such as that of a south wind. . . .[5]

The father is principle in a more excellent way than the mother, because he is the active principle, while the mother is a passive and material principle. Consequently, strictly speaking, the father is to be loved more. . . .[6]

Veneral pleasures above all debauch a man's mind, (and nothing) so casts down the manly mind from its height as the fondling of a woman.[7]

Gratian, a jurist from Bologna, said: The image of God is in man and it is one. Women were drawn from the man, who has God's jurisdiction as if he were God's vicar, because he has the image of the one God. Therefore woman is not made in God's image.[8]

Salimbene, a thirteen-century Franciscan, said: With flames of fire doth a woman sear the conscience of him who dwelleth by her.

Where women are with men, there shall be no lack of the devil's birdlime.

Woman was evil from the beginnings, a gate of death, a disciple of the servant, the devil's accomplice, a fount of deception, a dogstar to godly labours, rust corrupting the saints; whose perilous face hath overthrown such as had already become almost angels.[9]

Is it surprising that we have trouble bending to fit ourselves into traditional marriage roles and patterns based on teachings originating from people with the above beliefs?

However, the problems with traditional views on marriage are not only a narrow perspective and a negative view of sexuality and womankind. There is also an interpretive problem. The passages on marriage have not been examined in the light of good interpretive principles. One reason for this oversight is tied to our longstanding practices and teaching regarding women. We have, until recently, almost completely ignored Bible passages presenting women as equals to men in the church and showing them with abilities and opportunities far beyond the restricted realm the medieval church allowed them. And we did not examine Bible passages regarding women with good interpretive principles because it was easier to accept traditional interpretations. But now we have begun to explore that subject, and many of us believe the traditional interpretations were wrong. If the church has been wrong about the way it has treated women, could the church also have been wrong about the ideals and instructions it has traditionally taught about marriage? If it has misunderstood God's intention for women and their relationship to men, then very likely marriage, which is made up of women in relationship with men, was misunderstood too.

I believe the Bible presents a good case for equalitarian marriage: marriage based on equal persons using all they are and can be—first as individuals and then together harmoniously. I want to make it clear that I am not presenting just another formula and pat solution to all marriage problems. I am talking about a *principle* repeatedly evident in the New Testament both in instructions about marriage and about other relationships between believers, and exemplified in actions performed by Jesus to teach His own disciples how to relate to each other in the new family of faith. It is taking a principle—that of mutual submission of believers—and applying it to marriage. It is not a magical solution to all problems, but it will make a difference, a good and wholesome difference, as you will see if you choose to apply it to your own marriage.

I do not claim, as many do who encourage the traditional husband-over-wife hierarchy form of marriage, that God guarantees happiness or a successful marriage if you practice a more equal relationship. I do not think God guarantees any such thing anywhere regarding marriage. The best of efforts can be sabotaged by a marriage partner who has deep emotional problems and will not or cannot get help. But I believe there will be valuable information here even for someone married to an uncooperative and difficult spouse.

In the following chapters we will look at Bible passages on marriage and some tools for interpreting them. We will examine terms used to describe roles and positions traditionally thought necessary to a God-pleasing marriage—terms such as headship, submission, and obedience.

Equal marriage may sound startling and impractical at first. If it does, perhaps that is because you have always been taught that it is totally unworkable and directly opposed to God's plan. You may have never even seriously thought about such a marriage. I will be sharing with you information about how others have worked out the details of living together in an equal partnership, and I will be answering some questions you may have. We will look at ways to solve problems in an equal partnership and ways you can make changes if you want to.

But first let's look at marriage itself. Many books on marriage assume the reader and writer agree as to what marriage *is* and go on from there. I don't want to do that because some of our difficulties with marriage may come from a misunderstanding about what it is and can be. So instead of making assumptions, let's deal with this question: Just what is marriage anyway?

---

1. Susan Polis Schutz, *I Want to Laugh, I Want to Cry*, (Boulder, Colorado: Blue Mountain Arts, Inc., 1973), p. 20.

2. Lou Beardsley and Toni Spry, *The Fulfilled Woman* (Irvine, California: Harvest House, 1975), p. 23.

3. Erica Diamond, "A Fascinating Woman Gets Sprung or If Marabel Could Only See Me Now," *Free Indeed* (December/January 1978/79), p. 11.

4. Mary Daly, *The Church and the Second Sex* (New York: Harper and Row, 1968), p. 97.

5. Susan G. Bell, *Women from the Greeks to the French Revolution* (Belmont, California: Wadsworth Publishing Company, Inc., 1973), p. 122.

6. Vern L. Bullough and Bonnie Bullough, *The Subordinate Sex* (New York: Penguin Books, Inc., 1974), p. 175.

7. Ibid., p. 174.

8. Julia O'Faolain and Lauro Martines, eds., *Not in God's Image* (New York: Harper and Row, 1973), p. 130.

9. Bullough, *The Subordinate Sex*, p. 174.

HEIRS
HEIRS
HEIRS
HEIRS
HEIRS
HEIRS

TOGETHER

3

3

What Is Marriage?

Is marriage a holy sacrament permanently binding two individuals who were predestined for each other?

or

Is marriage merely a legal procedure to protect children and prevent the excesses of an immoral society?

or

Is marriage meant to be the happy union of a contented couple?

or

Is marriage a legal arrangement to cement a dynasty and ensure legitimate heirs to property?

or

Is marriage a relationship within which to express love and high regard?

or

Is marriage a safeguard to prevent the loosing of lust and licentiousness on the innocent and unconsenting?

or

Is marriage permanent?

or

Is marriage temporary?

Marriage is or has been everything mentioned above. It has been a private family arrangement throughout much of history, but for centuries it has also been a religious commitment for many. In modern America it is largely a civil matter.

There is a notion abroad now to the effect that marriage is no longer a genuine marriage when love is not present to cement the union. But that is not so. Marriage always has been a contract between two individuals, or their representatives, agreeing to a more or less permanent bond regardless of the love content. *It is just as much marriage when love is not present as when it is.* Marriage has often been more of a business transaction than a love match, but in spite of this it has still been a *personal relationship.* That is the only universal common ground of marriage—it is a relationship. Whether the atmosphere between the partners is pleasant, loving, or cool and distant, marriage is always a binding of two into a relationship.

The Basic Ingredient

We can look at marriage historically and culturally, practically and emotionally, but unless we examine it in the light of its basic element, as a relationship, we are bound to be confused and possibly diverted from finding direction we can use in our own marriages. If we try to follow a historical pattern for marriage originated with other people in other times, we may find that pattern unsuitable to our own times. We might have to squeeze ourselves out of shape to fit it. Copying the marriages of other cultures or images of marriage invented as practical innovations or romantic idealizations can be most uncomfortable and unprofitable for us. But if we focus on marriage as a relationship, we can then look for aids and information that we can apply to our own marriage relationship and know that we can use them or discard them on more realistic grounds than if we were trying to copy some ideal pattern.

Both the original creation account in Genesis 1 and the awe-struck meeting of Adam and Eve in Genesis 2 reflect God's intention that male and female would find their relationship satisfying and pleasurable. Adam immediately recognized the purpose of God's dual creation: "Ah! At last! Bone of my bone and flesh of my flesh!"

The Bible has much in it that is directly applicable to personal relationships. And it has information that is specifically about the relationship within marriage. Christians have focused so closely on marriage as an institution that we seem to have forgotten it is a relationship. We even give each other advice that is relationally destructive. We seem to have become preoccupied with a structure for marriage and forgotten the living relationship within it, just as Christians have so often become preoccupied with the organizational structure of the church and neglected the personal relationships between individual believers.

Seeking a Direction

Wives used to be captured in battle or purchased. A man might not be able to afford or capture the wife he really wanted so he would settle for what he could get.

Wives (and husbands) are often captured by pregnancy nowadays. Young women marry men who have impregnated them, even though under other circumstances they might not have chosen to marry that particular man. Men are often coerced or feel obligated to marry the women they have impregnated whether they would have chosen to do so under other circumstances or not.

People do not always marry the person they thought they were marrying. Jacob thought he was marrying Rachel,

the woman he loved. But when he lifted her veil, he found instead her sister, Leah. This happens today in a slightly different way. People are not always what they seem before they
marry. They put their best foot forward during courtship. The
other foot becomes obvious after the wedding ceremony and
the honeymoon. "I didn't know he/she was like that!" is
a common cry heard by marriage counselors, friends, and
parents.

Though we cannot always choose how our marriage will
begin and are often not aware of exactly whom we have married, we can choose what our marriage will *become* and who
we will become. I have a book on the shelf near me titled *If You
Don't Know Where You're Going You'll Probably End Up Some-
where Else.* That could be adapted to fit marriage: *If You Don't
Know What You Want Marriage To Be You'll Probably End Up
With Something Else.* People frequently have blind spots in
their thinking. They become so used to an uncomfortable situation that they assume they can do nothing about it. Many
people are unhappy about at least some situations in their
marriages, and yet they feel powerless to change anything.
They think, *that's what marriage does to you.* Or, *that's just the
way it is.*

Few couples even talk about what they want their marriage to be. They tend to let whatever happens happen, or they
may try to live out someone else's ideas about marriage. They
may copy their parents' marriages, consciously or uncon-
ciously. Many Christians will adopt a particular Christian
leader's ideas about marriage, assuming that that person
somehow knows more about marriage than they do. They
never even consider that *they* can determine what kind of marriage they want and then create it themselves.

But why not? It sounds revolutionary. Or maybe icono-
clastic is a better word. We don't think of marriage as something that is a do-it-yourself project. In the past it would
not have been easy or even possible to have the freedom to
make marriage what its participants wanted. We have that
freedom.

Dissatisfaction With Marriage

Marriage has been taking a beating recently. Some say it is a dead institution. Others say it is too restrictive. And many find it at least uncomfortable. It is as though marriage is an old shoe that doesn't fit any more. Some feel that in this case it is better just to go barefoot and do away with marriage altogether.

We can trace much of this dissatisfaction to a desire for the relationship in marriage to meet needs that were considered unimportant in the past. We expect different benefits from marriage. Then, women and men did not usually expect to have their closest personal relationships with their spouses. Marrriage provided other benefits: financial security, social position, children, care in sickness and old age, labor. When marriages were arranged by others or were contracted between a man and woman who did not know each other well before marriage, it seemed too much to demand that one's mate also be one's best friend. If love and close friendship developed, it was considered great good fortune, but was not necessarily expected. One's closest friends tended to be one's peers of the same sex or one's relatives.

We want more from marriage now in a close, personal way. We long for a relationship that is intimate and loving. A mate who is a good provider or a capable housekeeper and mother is not enough for us any more. We want a close friendship with our husband or wife.

This modern era is one of depersonalization. To our government we are numbers on social security cards. To our banks and credit card companies we are numbers in a computer. Our children stand in line to register for school and become numbers on other computer cards. We ride our interwoven, elaborate highways isolated from each other in individual cars. We are often alone even in groups. Feeling like nonpersons and numbers, we are hungry for meaningful human contact. Much of the personal identity and emotional well-being an individual realized in the past came from intimate contact with other people in work surroundings and while participating in the type of leisure activities that brought people together to interact with each other. Now even our leisure and recreational lives are isolated. We sit in our own rooms watching a television set. Or we jog alone along the road. Even when we are in a sports arena with thousands of other spectators, we do not touch or know each other.

This starvation for personal meaning and expression causes us to put an emotional overload on our marriages. We expect this relationship to make up the whole deficit. Usually there is not even an extended family to share it. Parents, grandparents, cousins, and other relatives are hundreds or thousands of miles away. We lose track of old friends and those we grew up with. Marriage is expected to fill almost all our interpersonal needs.

We must look at marriage in a new light if we expect it to survive this pressure. And we can look at it in a wiser light if we recognize that regarding marriage as an institutional pattern to fit one's self into rather than a relationship to feed and care for can never satisfy our longed-for need for intimacy.

An American Dissatisfaction

Rather than think that we Americans are wrestling unhappily with marriage solely because we are a degenerate society, let us consider some more honorable and more accurate reasons for our difficulties.

I am of English, Scots-Irish, Irish, German, Welsh, French and Cherokee extraction. And for an American that's not unusual. Most of the ancestors of modern Americans came from other countries only a few generations ago. Our forebears came to this country searching for a better life. They needed adequate food, shelter, and clothing. Above all, they wanted freedom—religious freedom, educational opportunity, and democratic freedom to choose their own government. Hard work and sustained effort secured those goals for them and ultimately for us. You and I have, thanks to our ancestors, the freedoms and opportunities they won for us all.

But the impetus that drove those pioneers and seekers

onward still lives in us and pushes us to reach further. Having the outward necessities, we now look inward. We want to know *ourselves* and realize our full individual potentials. Now we are able to move on to a wider freedom, the freedom to meet our personal emotional needs.

Looking inward, we see a need for intimate personal relationship. And yet, the means for meeting that need seem to be narrowing. While much has changed, marriage remains. It seems to represent both the security of the past and the hope for the future. But the marriage form of the past often thwarts our efforts for intimacy. We are trying to carry provisions for the present and future in inadequate containers from the past.

Looking for Solutions

We can attack the problem of the overload on marriage from several directions. We can work to make the marriage relationship itself a better vehicle for meeting our personal needs. But even if we do this, we must be realistic about what marriage can do. It cannot meet *every* need we have as individuals. We can take some of the load off marriage by reaching out to those around us and forming a sort of impromptu extended family of "adopted" relatives. This could help meet our needs for meaningful relationships outside marriage and at the same time reach out to other people who have similar needs. Some pastors are beginning to realize that the traditional church structure and form for services are not allowing their parishioners meaningful contact with each other. They are experimenting with ways believers may minister to each other and relate in small groups—to become family instead of a large, relatively impersonal social organization.

Those who would abolish marriage, discarding it as a useless institution, have identified some of the problems we are facing. They see the limitations marriage now has for so many. But they have the wrong solution. If we scrap marriage, we will still have our needs unmet, and will have destroyed the potential for close relationship which marriage *can* have if improved. If we try to find intimacy within a loose relationship substituting for marriage, a relationship that asks for no commitment and no continuity, we will frustrate that need again. For we humans require a personal security and confidence in our relationships that reaches beyond casual sex and "till we don't groove any more."

Let's not put marriage on the junk pile. Let's fix it. Let's make it what it has the potential to become. It seems strange that mature adults would not realize that if they can choose how they want to *live together* as an unmarried couple, they can also choose how they want to live together in a marriage.

We may have to throw out some preconceived notions about what marriage is and about what we have to be like in it. We can no longer expect to have some standard marriage behavior pattern handed to us in a package deal—not if we want our marriage to fit us. We will have to invent it ourselves. But never fear; we aren't totally on our own. There are guidelines in the Bible to help us build our own marriage.

Biblical Christianity and Equal Marriage

Information in the Bible tends to surface in time of need. We often do not see truth in Scripture until a particular need makes us sensitive to that truth's presence. I can read a psalm about help in time of trouble and appreciate it but not get anything special out of it. Yet when trouble comes and I read it again, it is alive for me in a new way, and I often see things in that passage I had missed before. It is that way in other areas too.

Present needs are forcing us to look at what the Bible says about marriage more carefully than we have before. In the past it was easier to live with the traditional interpretations of Bible passages on marriage because we could get by with less from marriage in a personal way.

Now we are searching more carefully those passages we had always taken for granted. Some are looking because of a personal need for a more satisfying marriage. Others have seen divorce tragedies and want to prevent both those obvious ordeals as well as the silent tragedy of a miserable marriage that is continued for any number of practical reasons but is only a shell surrounding a family of hurting, alienated people. They have looked at the traditional advice to married couples about roles and patterns and have found it to be inconsistent with other biblical principles. These inconsistencies have led them to deeper study and discoveries of what the Bible says about marriage relationships. This, in turn, has led them away from traditional hierarchical marriages and toward relationships of equal persons.

Like other unsought-for truths of the Bible that surface in time of need, these were there all along. The apostle Paul, writing to Christians in first-century Ephesus, gave instructions about how to live in their society in the new Way, the Christ Way. And those instructions can be used by us to discover how we, in this time and place, can live in our marriages according to the Christ Way. We are neither Ephesians nor first-century Greeks so we have to learn where we have similarities to them and where we have differences so that we will not misapply what God taught them and thus end up denying biblical truth in our lives though appearing to live it to the letter. First-century believers needed better relationships too, but for different reasons. Paul told them how to relate to one another as Christians, and his principles are timeless. Though we may not apply the principles exactly as an Ephesian Christian would have, the principles are for us too.

The principle of mutual submission of believers will work in any relationship, in any culture. Its purpose is to transcend culture and habit and make it possible for believers of every origin to relate as equal persons. I want to examine this principle and show how it can help a marriage become a relationship of equal persons who are able to use all they have, become all they can be, and enjoy and share the process.

But first, there may be questions about the roles we have been taught to follow. Are there traceable historical reasons for the marriage forms we have inherited? What forces created the impression among Christians that we must have a hierarchy of authority (chain of command) in marriage for it to be

"Christian?" Do we have to keep on doing things as we have always done them in order to be true to our faith? Is the foundation for the chain-of-command marriage biblical or historical?

We will be answering these questions as we look at the origins of hierarchical rules and patterns for marriage in the next chapter.

HEIRS
TOGETHER

4

Is There a Divine Order for Marriage?

Habit has given permanence to errors, which ignorance had previously rendered universal.[1]

You will be told by many people that the modification in our attitude towards the relations between men and women endangers the sanctity of that relation. The reverse is, I maintain, the case. The substitution of intelligence for the authority of tradition endangers the tragedy of unhappy marriages. It endangers nothing else; it makes, on the contrary, the realisation of the ideal of marriage more attainable than it could ever have been before. Marriage has rested upon economic conditions, it has rested upon traditional and romantic sentiments. It is to be hoped that it will rest in the future to a larger extent than in the past upon intelligence and justice.[2]

Among Christians several beliefs prevail so widely that it is assumed by most that they derive directly from Scripture. But though these ideas may harmonize with biblical truth, they come from conclusions drawn by persons of a particular theological persuasion; they do not come directly from the Bible.

For example, many Christians believe that God has a distinct plan for each individual's life and that one should endeavor to find that plan and stay within it. One's chief goal in life becomes finding God's unique plan and not straying from it. These Christians feel a specific plan for them exists that is so final and complete that it is all but written and sealed. Along the same line is the belief that there is a "direct will of God" and a "permissive will of God," the second being less than the best. Now, you will have a hard time digging up any Scripture passages that directly refer to either belief. This is not to say they are wrong. Whether they are valid assumptions or not is not my point. They may or may not be. But the fact is that they are *assumptions* that derive from a particular theological stance. They are logical extensions of a view of God as sovereign. They are theological interpretations of the biblical evidences, if you will, that lead to the belief in a plan for one's life predetermined by God and the belief in a direct will and a permissive will of God.

If we would trace the history of theological and denominational movements within Christianity, we could probably track these ideas back to their beginnings. I mention them merely to illustrate the prevalence of such ideas within Christendom and to emphasize the fact that they have traceable sources and that it is natural and normal for such assumptions to exist.

Another assumption commonly accepted among Christians is that there is a divinely ordained order for the human family, and more particularly for marriage. It is called a hierarchy or "chain of command." This belief is so widely accepted among believers that it is seldom questioned at all. Most evangelicals assume this order is firmly supported by the Bible so they do not consider questioning it. If they have difficulties applying this order to their own lives, they assume they are somehow at fault because it couldn't possibly be the order itself causing the problem.

But this "divine order" for marriage also has a traceable history. Some of its roots go back to the intricate theology of the medieval church. Others extend into early asceticism which arose in the first several centuries of the Christian Era. Other factors fed and helped form this traditional view of marriage requiring a hierarchical chain of command within the family.

Several of the factors contributing to this belief have to do with historical attitudes toward and beliefs about women taught by the church. Many of the Bible passages traditionally interpreted to restrict women's ministry within the church and their freedom of participation within society at large were also foundations for the belief in an order of command within the family. These passages have been long neglected by Bible scholars because the almost complete exclusion of women from serious Bible study created a limited perspective within the scholarly world. It was easy for male scholars to be blind to problems and inconsistencies that did not touch them or parallel in any way their own experience.

A similar situation existed in the case of slavery. Often white churchmen and theologians were not sensitive to the black experience. They saw no problem with the interpretations of Scripture that supported slavery. And since black Christians had neither access to the tools of hermeneutics nor voice to speak out and make the inconsistencies known, there was a long silence. Now we can see the historical roots within medieval theology that have given us a heritage of church-supported oppression of blacks, oppression justified by Bible passages that were misinterpreted.

In this chapter we will examine some of the historical influences that formed the traditional marriage roles so widely accepted by Christians today. In later chapters we will look at the biblical evidence, using better interpretative principles than the ones used by the medieval formulators of the divine-order belief.

The Early Church's Attitude Toward Women

Jesus' treatment of women was genuinely revolutionary for His time and culture. He never referred to women or treated them in any of the stereotypical ways common to His contemporaries. Within His culture women were believed to be inferior, temptations to men who should be hidden and generally ignored. Women were considered primarily as sexual temptations. The first century woman suffered from all the sins of the underdog, but it was assumed these came from her nature, not her status. *The Universal Jewish Encyclopedia* states:

> The beauty of women had always been a snare to the instincts of men. The Midrash explains that Eve was created after Adam so that he could be reminded, when he complained about her, that it was he who had prayed to God to create a companion for him. Abel's beautiful wife was one of the main causes of strife between him and his brother Cain. The Talmud records the prayer of an exceptionally beautiful girl that men should not be led to sinful thoughts by her beauty. A man is not allowed to recite certain prayers in the presence of a woman who is not fully dressed.[3]

Women were not permitted to serve as witnesses, and yet Jesus chose women as the first witnesses to His resurrection. Jesus treated women as *people.* He went out of His way to refute by His actions the attitudes toward women reflected in the above quote. He insisted Mary of Bethany be allowed to sit at His feet and learn theology instead of being sent to the kitchen where custom would have placed her. He raised the woman taken in adultery to the human level of her accusers. The woman of Samaria was as surprised as His disciples that He would talk to her, a woman. But Jesus went further; He commissioned her to bring the Good News to her whole village.

Though His male disciples showed surprise at His treatment of women, they finally accepted women as coparticipants in the faith. The wide scope of participation of women in both public and private ministry is evident in the Book of Acts and in the Epistles. The New Testament reveals an infant church in which all shared regardless of sexual, racial, social, or ethnic differences. But the situation changed early in the history of the church. There was a gradual decline in women's participation, until by the sixth century all ministering women were finally forced into cloisters.

The question, of course, is: Why? What happened? The restriction of women early in the history of the church has a bearing on our own attitudes toward marriage, so it is important for us to know what did happen.

The Influence of Asceticism

Throughout the East in the first century, new religions and cultic practices were being tasted and incorporated into the old religions or were beginning to supplant them. Soldiers of the Roman Empire had brought back from their far-flung military campaigns news about new religions and philosophies. One of the philosophies that became popular at the time was Gnosticism.

> The extreme form of the prevailing Hellenistic world view is known as Gnosticism, a redemptive religion based on a radical dualism, beginning with the understanding new to the ancient world of the utter difference of human existence from the world. Salvation comes through knowledge (gnosis) of the heavenly origin of the self, a knowledge which gives the Gnostic his consciousness of superiority to the world. This sense of superiority could be expressed through a strict asceticism, denying the body and its lusts, or through a condescending libertinism, demonstrating emancipation from all moral conventions. These two tendencies are, of course, intimately related and both are to be found in the early church.[4]

Gnostic beliefs made inroads into all the major religions of the day. Both Judaism and Christianity struggled against Gnostic teaching. Since one of the tenets of the Gnostic philosophy was that the physical body was evil, they believed that to feed the good (the spirit) one should deny the body and suppress its desires. Another branch of Gnosticism held that since the body was evil anyway, it did not matter what one did with one's body. They excused any manner of physical excess that was desired.

The infant church struggled against Gnosticism for a long time. At one stage it looked as though biblical Christianity would succumb to the dualism of Gnostic thought and be per-

manently deflected from its purpose. But by the end of the
third century the battle for orthodoxy had largely been
won—with one remnant of the Gnostic influence remaining.
That remaining influence was asceticism.

Denial of the physical body and its desires became a way
for the faithful to gain spiritual merit. The excesses of the desert
monks in pursuing self-denial and degradation were amazing.
They lived on the barest rations of unappetizing food; some
never washed, even living in their own excrement. It became
apparent that some desires were harder to eradicate than others,
and monks found sexual desires the hardest to deal with and
obliterate. Some went to the extent of self-castration to rid
themselves of sexual thoughts. Eventually they came to the conclusion that sexual desires were the most evil, and it was only
a step further to decide that the object of those desires was the
chief evil. Thus, women were regarded as tempters of the pure.

It became obvious to those holding this view that it was
not proper to give positions of public ministry to such poten-
tially dangerous persons. So, gradually women had their new
freedoms in Christ removed from them.

Theologians posited rationales for these restrictions.

> *St. John Chrysostom* said: The woman taught once, and
> ruined all. On this account . . . let her not teach. But what
> is it to other women that she suffered this? It certainly
> concerns them; for the sex is weak and fickle.[5]

> *The Jurist Gratian* said: Woman's authority is nil; let her in
> all things be subject to the rule of man. . . . And neither
> can she teach, nor be a witness, nor give a guarantee, nor
> sit in judgment.[6]

Women were seen as persons needing firm control to keep
them from doing damage to the pious.

> *Clement of Alexandra* said: Nothing disgraceful is proper
> for man, who is endowed with reason; much less for
> woman, to whom it brings shame even to reflect of what
> nature she is. . . . By no manner of means are women to
> be allowed to uncover and exhibit any part of their person,
> lest both fall—the men by being excited to look, they by
> drawing on themselves the eyes of men.[7]

Women who entirely suppressed their sexual natures could serve God providing they were cloistered from the eyes of the world and separated from men. Women who remained in the secular world were to be under the control of either fathers, husbands, or sons. The church adopted the negative attitude toward women that had been rampant in the first century world before Jesus came with His Good News. Women were seen as possessing a fatal flaw, as incomplete, as evil. The church reverted to this world view.

This restriction and repression of women had a twofold effect that is still in evidence today. First of all, it guaranteed that women could not be equal participants in the teaching ministry of the church. They were not educated in skills fitting them for Bible interpretation, and they were considered incomplete humans, and as such they could not represent God in the pulpit or study. As Augustine said:

> The woman herself alone is not the image of God: whereas the man alone is the image of God as fully and completely as when the woman is joined with him.[8]

Excluding women from Bible interpretation helped perpetuate those early errors regarding women, for the woman's experience could not motivate her to further study that would bring the truth to light. Women had neither the tools to interpret nor the forum or voice to reveal the truth even if they could find it.

The second effect was that this attitude toward women bred a belief that women *must* be governed by men in order to prevent evil and chaos. And if you listen today to the arguments for a chain of command in marriage, you will hear this reflected: *someone must* rule in marriage. The assumption is always that the woman *needs* rule.

The Medieval Order of Things

"A place for everything, and everything in its place," was my friend Minnie Ten Kley's answer when I asked if it was hard to fit her family comfortably into their mobile home. That good, practical Dutch advice is also a perfect summary of the medieval church's not so good nor practical solution to *every* problem. The church believed everything and everyone had a place, and it determined what that place would be and used force if necessary to keep everything and everyone in place.

During the medieval era the church was not merely a religious body giving out spiritual food and solace. It was a giant politico-religious juggernaut that rolled over anyone who dared to differ with it. The church was the final authority on all matters, including the natural world, human nature, spiritual truths, and movements of the heavenly bodies.

Over a length of time the church had evolved a vast system of "truths" that explained everything from angels to rain. This body of truth was arrived at not by the scientific method of observation and experimentation (this method was considered heretical and blasphemous) but by theologians reasoning theologically on assembled passages of Scripture. By this method they determined that rain was let down to the earth through literal windows in heaven by angels who opened and closed them by hand. They also determined that there were successive layers of transparent spheres encircling the earth which had embedded in them the sun, moon, planets, and stars. These spheres revolved about a stationary earth which was firmly fixed on an actual foundation. Man (male) was the center of the universe, and woman was firmly under his governance.

In this great plan everyone had a place. Order was maintained when each person stayed in his or her place and did the job that went with the position God had ordained. Some people were born to serve (slave races), while others were born to reign (divine right of kings). Even prostitution had a place in this order. Augustine's earlier comments had foreshadowed and contributed to this intricate system:

> What is more base, empty of worth, and full of vileness than harlots and other such pests? Take away harlots from human society and you will have tainted everything with lust. Let them be with the matrons and you will produce contamination and disgrace. So this class of persons, on account of their morals, of a most shameless life, fills a most vile function under the laws of order.[9]

Based on this same process, there were remedies for all manner of ills. For pain and sickness, prayer was the solution. Painkilling herbs and opiates used before the church gained power were now forbidden on the grounds that their use showed a lack of faith; thus, they must be of Satan and not God. Storms were to be stopped by the ringing of church bells because this would frighten Satan (the prince and power of the air) and he would leave and take his storm also.

This Divine Order of Things seems silly to us now. It is hard to believe that intelligent people, especially those who had access to the Bible, could believe such nonsense, let alone punish and torture those who disagreed. But they did.

One well-known example of the measures Christians took to defend this order is the case of Galileo. He made the mistake of looking through his telescope and seeing the phases of Venus. He realized the Earth did move after all, and he proceeded to tell others that it did. For this he was threatened with the Inquisition, forced to deny what he knew to be true, and exiled. His works were destroyed and his name besmirched throughout the civilized world. Roman Catholic and Protestant leaders alike denounced Galileo's observation as satanic and blasphemous. The reason: it contradicted the very foundation of the Divine Order of Things.

The Protestant Reformation did not disrupt the belief in this order. The list of the defenders of the Order of Things against the Copernican theory which Galileo espoused reads like a Who's Who of Protestant history.

> *Martin Luther:* "People give ear to an upstart astrologer who strove to show that the earth revolves, not the heavens or the firmament, the sun and the moon. Whoever wishes to appear clever must devise some new system, which of all systems is of course the very best. This fool wishes to reverse the entire science of astronomy; but sacred Scripture tells us that Joshua commanded the sun to stand still, not the earth."
>
> *Melanchthon:* "The eyes are witnesses that the heavens revolve in the space of twenty-four hours. But certain men, either from the love of novelty, or to make a display

of ingenuity, have concluded that the earth moves; re-
volves. . . . Now, it is a want of honesty and decency to
assert such notions publicly, and the example is perni-
cious. It is the part of a good mind to accept the truth as
revealed by God and to acquiesce in it."

John Calvin: "Who will venture to place the authority of
Copernicus above that of the Holy Spirit?"

John Owen: "Delusive and arbitrary hypothesis, contrary
to Scripture."

John Wesley said the new ideas "tend toward infidelity."[10]

All these leaders concluded that the *inspiration* of the
Scriptures was at issue, never realizing it was their *interpretations* of the Scriptures that were in error, interpretations that
were part of the necessary building blocks of the Divine Order
of Things. Their acceptance of the order as infallible blinded
them to the error of the separate interpretations supporting it.

Finally, Copernicus was vindicated. The church pulled
back from its immovable stance and admitted it was wrong in
the interpretations of the Scriptures it had used to insist the
Earth was firmly fixed on an actual physical foundation. But it
held fast to other parts of the order until similarly forced to
give them up. For example, slavery was vociferously defended
by many churchmen. Again they claimed the issue at stake
was the inspiration of the Scriptures, and again they eventually had to give up their interpretations of passages they had
used to support slavery as part of God's divine order. The
divine right of kings stood until democracy forced a reexamin-
ation of the passages which had been falsely interpreted.

But one part of the Divine Order of Things still stands.
That part is "God's plan for marriage," or as some call it, the
"chain of command." It was part and parcel of the medieval
Order of Things, and its foundation was just as shaky as those
holding up the other parts of that vast system evolved by
medieval theologians and supported by misused Scripture. Yet
it is still held on to by those who insist that to question this
order for the family is to question the inspiration of the Bible.

In the next chapter we will talk about some principles of
biblical interpretation that are now accepted by almost all who

seriously study the Bible. These principles can be used to measure the interpretative accuracy of the claims supporting the remnant of the Order of Things that still stands. In other chapters we will look at pertinent Bible passages and use these principles of Bible interpretation. But before we go on to interpretative matters, we should discuss two other factors that have affected our ideas about what Christian marriage should be. These two factors are interrelated: the overwhelming social changes caused by the industrial revolution and the resulting ideals of the Victorian era.

The Industrial Revolution

Prior to the industrial revolution most manufacturing of goods was done in homes as cottage industry. Women shared in both the work and management of such business. They might be poor women working alone or with their own small family, or they might be wealthy women with many servants and a large estate to manage. Often men were away from the family business and holdings for long stretches of time during which the work and property were managed by wives and mothers. The frequent wars and crusades made it necessary for women to take charge or continue the work they had always done in management.

Even though women were denied political and religious equality with men, they did have the means for self-support by plying a trade or managing the family business. Their work covered almost every trade or occupation. The *Book of Husbandry* from the fifteenth century gives an indication of the scope of a woman's expertise and earning potential:

> In the begynynge of Marche, or a lyttell afore, is tyme for a wyfe to make her garden, and to gette as many good sedes and herbes as she canne, and specially suche as be good for the potte, and to eate . . . let thy dystaffe be always redye for a pastyme, that thou be not ydle. . . .
>
> It is convenyente for a housbande to have shepe of his owne, for many causes, and than maye his whfe have some part of the woll, to make her husbande and herselfe some clothes. And at the least waye, she may have the

lockes of the shepe, eyther to make clothes or blankettes
and coverlettes, or bothe. And if she have no woll of her
owne, she maye take woll to spynne of clothmakers, and
by that means may have a convenyent lyvynge, and many
tymes to do other workes. It is a wyves occupation, to
wynower all maner of cornes, to make malte, to wasshe
and wrynge, to make heye, shere corne, and in tyme of
nede to helpe her husbande to fyll the muck-wayne or
doung-carte, dryve the ploughe, to loode hey, corne, and
suche other. And to go or ride to the market, to sel butter,
shese, mylke, egges, chekyns, capons, hennes, pygges,
gese, and all manyr of cornes. And also to bye all maner of
necessarye thynges belongynge to housholde, and to make
a trewe rekenynge and a-compte to her housbande, what
she hath payed.[11]

The woman of Proverbs 31, the "virtuous woman," was a
manager and worker in the family business, thus freeing her
husband for political position "in the gates."

As Boulding explains in *The Underside of History:*

Women's economic partnership roles throughout history
deserve more attention. Recent research indicates that the
capital available to women in their domestic partner role,
through dowry, inheritance, and management of production activities was considerably larger than hitherto
realized. . . . Their use of this capital in civic projects also
has not been recognized. With the industrial revolution
and the shrinking of domestic productivity down to
one-fourth to one-fifth or less of the total productivity of a
society, capital available to women also shrank and non-
domestic worksites became more important. That shrink-
age was accompanied by political changes that abolished
the public roles of elite women, compounding economic
deprivation with political deprivation at the very time
when new ideals of political participation were develop-
ing. The old household partnership model could no longer
serve, and industrialization seemed to spell disaster for
women. (p. 10).[12]

The balance of partnership that did exist within the home of
the past was destroyed by the taking of a woman's work out to
a factory or business to which she must go and work for
another to earn her living or help earn the family's living.

> When with spinning, weaving, knitting, churning, pickling, curing, and preserving, the home was a workshop, the wife was not "supported" by her husband. He knew the value of her contribution and took her seriously, even if he did belittle her opinions on politics and theology. But, with the industrial decay of the home, it is more and more often the case that the husband "supports" his wife.[13]

The industrial revolution's centralization of production in factories and cities and its removal of manufacturing from the woman's realm reduced her value and made it impossible for her to manage the home, care for her family, and make a living wage also. Home was no longer a place to work together and teach the next generation the family trade. Home life, as it had been, was shattered, and the woman was left without the means to carry on her work successfully. Now she must choose, if she could, to work for wages or stay at home and send others out. Many had no choice, for the industrial revolution created a new kind of class society. Those who had been able to be self-supporting now became the bottom rung of the socio-economic ladder, the very poor who must live on the pitifully low wages they could get from the factory in order to survive at all.

Previously, women had been able to be self-supporting, even when alone; their dependence upon men had been legal but not economic. Now this was no longer possible. What had been the location of the family business was often just a place to sleep at night. For the rising middle class, the newly moneyed in this changing social order, a place was created for a new kind of woman, the Victorian lady.

The Victorian Era

In a time when rapid social and ideological change was eating away at the fabric of family and private life, the home was increasingly seen as the last bastion of refuge. Home became the place where one could escape from the world of clanging machines, rationalizations that denied former values, and challenges to religious beliefs. Home became a haven, and woman's narrowing sphere was given a new meaning and value by this sentimentalizing of home. She became its keeper.

The Victorian era was saturated with sentimentality. Religion was seen increasingly in a sentimentalized light and as something women were more prone to than men (directly contrary to the views of the past). Womanhood became a symbol for purity and truth. There was dichotomy in everything: public and private life, truth and sentimentality, rational and moral. Victorian middle-class women became the embodiment of all that was good and pure and worth preserving. They represented *home*. In past centuries women had been regarded as base, inferior, sensual, and licentious. Now they became pure, morally superior, fragile, and asexual.

> The "true woman" is almost incapable of feeling sexuality, and sexual desire is banished from her mind. Carnality is ceded to the male nature, as part of his rough dealings with the "real world" of materialism and power. Religion likewise recedes into the "feminine" world of spirituality divorced from truth or power. The material world is now seen as the "real world," the world of hard, practical aggressivity, devoid of sentiment or morality. [14]

But there was dichotomy here too. The position of the Victorian ladies at the top was balanced by another class of women at the bottom of the economic scale. Poor women, unable to stay at home and maintain a refuge from the world, were forced to work double shift—one at the factory, another at home.

> Fall River gave me another view of what the Industrial Revolution had done to women. In the cotton mills whole families worked together, mostly the same tasks and always the same hours. All worked, but when the whistles blew and the toilers poured out of the mills and hurried to their homes, what happened? The women of the mills went on working. They cooked and served meals, washed dishes, cleaned the house, tucked the children into bed, and after that sewed, mended or did a family washing. Eleven o'clock at night seemed the conventional hour for clothesline pulleys to begin creaking all over town. . . . In Fall River a woman in the mills and at home worked an

average of fourteen hours a day and had babies between times. The babies could not be taken to the mills, and as soon as the mothers were able to leave their beds they relegated the care of the babies to some grandmother, herself a broken down mill-worker, or to the baby-farms in which the town abounded. Of course the babies fared ill under this system, the mortality rate among them being very high. In summer, a reputable physician told me, it sometimes reached the appalling rate of 50 percent of all births. . . . The whole panorama of women's lives in that mill-town gave me the impression that the human race was on its way to the abyss.[15]

Many unmarried women could not adequately support themselves on the low factory wages and were forced into prostitution. Thus, prostitution flourished because of the desperate situation of the poor working woman and because of the attitude toward sexuality in the upper and middle classes. Men could not express their sexual feelings with "good" women and so turned to the poor woman who was desperate enough to sell her body in order to survive. These women were then regarded as inferior, depraved, animal-like, and deserving of such treatment.

Since the working woman was often sexually exploited while the exploiter's sheltered wife stayed safely at home, a negative attitude developed toward working women. As one historian states: "Since the cult of true womanhood made the leisured woman normative, women going to work could only be viewed as a downfall from the sanctity of home."[16] Regardless of the kind of work a woman might do, paid work itself signified degradation.

The Victorian era has passed, yet there is still the lingering conviction that a woman working away from home violates that home and is a step down for both the woman and the home itself. This attitude is reflected in the way working hours and requirements are set up. In spite of the fact that 40 percent* of our work force is female, "the world of work still organizes itself as though workers are male and have nonworking wives providing for their domestic needs."[17]

*Recent statistics say 50 percent.

The church has frequently been last in line to understand and adapt positively to social change, and such is the case here. We are still operating under the assumption that the Victorian-lady ideal was a biblical image of what a good woman should be. We know so little of our collective history that we assume our recent history is the norm we should work to maintain, not realizing it is a distortion forced upon us by a social situation and an economic upheaval that changed the shape of the family and society in the space of a few years.

The Effects of Social Change

We are now experiencing more social change and new developments that give rise to the same kinds of apprehensions and insecurities brought on by the industrial revolution. And we are inclined to do what our ancestors did. We are trying to hold on to some of the values from our past by institutionalizing them in the home. We want life to stay the way we remember it from a generation ago when the world seemed simpler, better, more understandable. To do this, we are prepared to preach a modified version of the Victorian-lady ideal to our women. We reach back to the Divine Order of Things from medieval theology and use it to justify insisting that women behave in stereotypical ways taken from another era. We want to preserve values; instead, we only create roles and rules to live by that neither fit our needs today nor accurately reflect our values.

During a time of rapid social change, people always try to hold on to the past with one hand while reaching toward the future with the other. They cling to certain forms and structures because those forms and structures make them feel safe and comfortable. But inappropriate and rigid forms eventually become so uncomfortable that they are gradually modified by most people. The danger for Christians in these situations is that they become so preoccupied with forms and blind to the reasons they hold to them that they are unable to apply timeless Christian principles to new situations in healing, helping ways. They are too tempted to put their trust in pat answers and false issues. Ignoring the true issues, they are unable to find workable and reasonable answers.

Wouldn't it be more appropriate to reach back to the New Testament and its time and look for principles taught there which can help believers deal with the situations they face in their society? We cannot keep social change from happening. We cannot fit the marriages of the present into the worn and ill-fitting garments of the past. But we can use biblical principles, applying them to our contemporary situation, and find answers; we can live biblically and successfully in our marriages now.

The New Testament focuses on the relationship, not the form or the roles or the structure or the maintaining of the status quo.

1. Charles Brockden Brown, *Alcuin: A Dialogue* (New York: Grossman, 1970), pp. 13-14.

2. M. F. Ashley Montagu, ed., *Marriage Past and Present* (Boston: Porter Sargent, 1956) pp. 61-62.

3. Isaac Landminn, ed., *The Universal Jewish Encyclopedia* (New York: Universal Jewish Encyclopedia, Inc., 1943), 10:566.

4. Lloyd Gaston and James Lindenberger, "Marriage and the Biblical Style," *Theology* (Winter 1976/77), p. 7.

5. O'Faolain and Martines, *Not in God's Image*, p. 129.

6. Ibid., p. 130.

7. Ibid., p. 133.

8. Augustine, *De Trinitate* 7:7, 10.

9. Augustine, *De Ordine*, as quoted in *Folkways* by William Graham Sumner (Dover, 1906), pp. 529-530.

10. A. D. White, *A History of the Warfare of Science with Theology in Christendom* (New York: Dover Publications, 1960), 1:127-128.

11. Margaret Isabel Cole, *Marriage Past and Present* (London: J. M. Dent & Sons, 1938), p. 80.

12. Elise Boulding, *The Underside of History* (Boulder, Colorado: Westview Press, 1976), p. 10.

13. Anne Firor Scott, ed., *The American Woman: Who Was She?* (Englewood Cliffs, New Jersey: Prentice-Hall, Inc., 1971), p. 131.

14. Walter Burkhardt, ed., *Woman: New Dimensions* (New York: Paulist Press, 1977), p. 78.

15. Scott, *The American Woman*, pp. 19-20.

16. Burkhardt, *Woman*, p. 79.

17. Ibid., pp. 79-80.

HEIRS
HEIRS
HEIRS
HEIRS
HEIRS
HEIRS

TOGETHER

5

Helps for Understanding Bible Passages on Marriage

I think it would be very easy to start a new religious cult. You could just pick up your Bible and locate some verse that *sounds like* what you want to teach; then insist that is *exactly* what it means, ignoring all other biblical evidence to the contrary. Be rigid and dogmatic about it, and you would soon have followers. If anyone challenged your ideas, you could point to the passage and say, *"But that is what it says!"*

It is almost as easy to be a quickie Bible interpreter. And sometimes almost as damaging. Most of the material in the Bible is easy to understand and poses no problem for the average Christian. You read it and you know how to live it. But there are areas in Scripture where it is necessary to have more interpretive skill than just common sense, though that is an extremely helpful commodity for a Bible interpreter to possess.

In keeping with this, we will look first at some basic principles of Bible interpretation upon which almost everyone who seriously studies the Bible can agree. Then we will look at additional data that will help us understand what marriage was like for people who lived during the time the New Testament was written. If we know what marriage was like for them, we can better understand the advice and instruction written to them by the New Testament writers. We will then be able to apply that instruction for our own benefit.

Principles of Bible Interpretation

In school the subject is called *hermeneutics*. Without a knowledge of good hermeneutics you can go pretty far afield in Bible interpretation. We looked at the hermeneutics of the medieval theologians in the last chapter. Fortunately, there have been some improvements in hermeneutical principles since then. Unfortunately, they are not always used even by those who know good hermeneutics. But you can use them yourselves to study the Bible. I'll be using them in later chapters when we examine Bible passages on marriage.

Bible Interpretation (Hermeneutical) Principles

Always interpret a passage in agreement with its context. This is probably the most frequently violated and ignored principle of interpretation. The *context* of a passage is its surrounding verses and chapters. If we take a verse out of context, as though neatly clipping it out with scissors, it can sound as though it means something (sometimes several things) that it does not mean at all.

Supporting a view by using verses that have been ripped from their contexts is called *prooftexting*. That sounds nasty and deliberate, but it is a common, innocent enough occurrence. For example, a person studying for a Sunday school lesson might get the Bible, turn to the concordance in the back, look up all the references to a certain word, read all the verses listed, and draw conclusions based upon reading those verses (totally ignoring their individual contexts). This method is much like the one the medieval church scholars used to determine that the earth did not move. Most of the time people will not draw such far-out conclusions, nor are they apt to send anyone to the Inquisition for disagreeing with them. However, they are still in danger of misinterpreting what God was actually saying in those verses. And to do so is to miss what He would say to them, and possibly lead both themselves and others to a wrong conclusion on the matter.

This context-ignoring, or prooftexting, is also the way of the cultist, as I mentioned earlier. We must take into account the surrounding verses and chapters to be sure we have enough information to insist a verse means what we think it means at first glance.

Interpret a passage in the light of its probable meaning to the persons for whom it was originally written. This principle helps us understand that just because Jesus washed the disciples' feet doesn't mean we have to do that too. In those days, washing a guest's feet was a social custom of welcome and hospitality. Therefore, we apply the spirit of their custom to our own time and show our willingness to do humble service for each other in ways that would be meaningful to us now.

It also makes a holy kiss unnecessary as a greeting. As a teen-ager, I once embarrassed myself in front of a whole gathering by quoting "greet the brethren with a holy kiss" as the admittance requirement to a youth meeting. The fellow at the door asking for a verse was tolerant, and I thought it would be a clever response. (And he *was* handsome.) But I didn't know all those in the next room could hear my quote. I didn't get my kiss, holy or otherwise (didn't expect I would,) but I didn't forget the experience either. My welcomer and I both knew that a holy kiss was the way the brethren greeted each other with Christian love in the first century, but now we in the U.S. shake hands.

When interpreting a passage, consider the customs and events taking place when it was written. This principle overlaps the one just mentioned. Knowledge of customs of the first century is often the key to explaining difficult verses, while acquaintance with historical events in the first century world can be important in helping extract the full meaning from many passages. For example, in 1 Peter we read that believers were to obey those who ruled over them. What must be known to accurately apply that passage is that the people to whom that was written were under Roman rule, a fundamentally just rule, if harsh. The instruction was to a people who had a government they could in good conscience obey; they were not living under an evil regime like that of Nazi Germany. Therefore, to apply that passage to all governments for all time and bind the Christian to mindless, conscienceless civil obedience is to violate this interpretive principle, for knowing the events of the first century limits the application of this passage to governments that are also just.

To use another example, it helps us understand Paul's instructions in 1 Corinthians on abstaining from marriage if we know about the persecutions Christians were beginning to experience at that time. Paul was not saying he was against marriage, but he was saying that marriage would make believers' lives more complicated, with more dependents and family members to leave fatherless, motherless, husbandless, or wifeless if they were killed. Thus, he advised against marrying because of the times in which they lived.

Interpret a passage in the light of all other Scripture. When I was in high school, I had a friend who belonged to a denomination which believed baptism was necessary for salvation. I, being of Baptist background and conviction, was sure that salvation was by faith alone and that baptism was only the outward testimony to the inward change. But my friend would have none of that. He opened his Bible to Mark 16:16 and read, or rather had me read for myself, "He that believeth and is baptized shall be saved."

"See," he said, "that's what it says and that's what it means. You have to be baptized to be saved."

I proceeded to try to reason with him about it, bringing in other Bible verses that talked about belief and grace, not works. No use. He was steadfast. Every scriptural proof I cited was met with his Bible thrust before me and, "What does it say?" It was that same verse over and over again.

I remember leaving the conversation puzzled and wondering why all my proofs were of no interest to him. Years later

I learned about Bible interpretation and identified the principle that was at issue.

Do not use an obscure passage to disprove one with clear and obvious meaning. This principle also overlaps somewhat with the previous one. There are instances when we come upon a passage that is extremely difficult to understand. For these rare passages we may have to conclude that we lack data (that we may yet unearth) to completely unlock the meaning. With some other passages we can pose several possibilities as to what they *may* mean.

The careful Bible student does not just toss these difficult passages away as useless, but he or she does use them with an awareness of their difficulties. And one thing the careful student docs not do is use a difficult, obscure passage to overturn or contradict another passage with clear and problem-free interpretation.

First Timothy 2:11–15 is one of those difficult passages. It says:

> Let a woman learn quietly with complete submission. I do not allow a woman to teach, neither to domineer over a man; instead, she is to keep still. For Adam was first formed, then Eve. And Adam was not deceived, but the woman, since she was deceived, experienced the transgression. She will, however, be kept safe through the childbearing, if with self-control she continues in faith and love and consecration (MLB).

A few days ago I sat and listened to a man insist that this passage must be used to interpret Genesis 2 as creating an "order of command" even though the Genesis passage contains no hint of such a thing in itself. He also used this passage to limit the meaning of other passages of Scripture that show women participating freely in the early church.

The question, of course, is what *do* you do with a passage like this? It *seems* to say that women cannot teach because of Adam and Eve, that women are saved through bearing children, or that women are kept alive during childbirth because they have lived a particular kind of holy life. These ideas are all contrary to much of what the Bible teaches elsewhere.

The principle stated at the beginning of this section should cause us to look upon passages such as this as portions we should study carefully and refuse to use dogmatically. We do not ignore them or toss them out; we interpret them carefully with full awareness that we do not have enough data to completely unravel their meaning—at least not at this point. So rather than use them to change what is obviously taught elsewhere, we will look for more information. But that is not all we can do with such a problem passage. We can use the available data and pose possible interpretations that do not violate sound interpretive principles. Allowing for more than one meaning for such a passage can often shed light and help us understand the passage even though we cannot be certain what its exact meaning is.

In the case of 1 Timothy 2:11–15 there are at least four, possibly more, interpretations that do not violate sound Bible study principles.[1]

1. This portion may refer to women disrupting the public meetings, as they did in Corinth (1 Cor. 14:34–35), to carry on discussions or argue with their husbands. Paul may be citing a commonly accepted Jewish saying, "Adam was first formed," to remind them that this behavior was considered disrespectful and therefore unacceptable. The last part of the passage may be saying that women are exonerated from Eve's part in the fall by the "birth of the child" (Christ.)

2. There may have been two kinds of services in the early church—one was public where unbelievers could observe and another was private for believers only. Women may have been prevented from participating in the public meetings because for them to do so would have been scandalous to Greek pagan observers. In the private meetings women would have been allowed full participation and use of their gifts of preaching and teaching (as indicated by other passages).

3. There may have been two kinds of teaching at that time. One kind of teaching may have involved the argumentation that was common in synagogue worship. For women to argue with their husbands in public would have been as out-

rageous in both Greek and Jewish society as a man's slave arguing with him. So women would have been barred from that type of teaching ministry for propriety's sake.

4. Another possibility which is more involved but perhaps the most likely meaning of the passage is that this was a local situation in which Paul was limiting the participation of women for a time until they had learned Christian doctrine. Then they would not be so prone to being led astray by false teachers and subsequently using the believers' assembly to perpetuate these false teachings.

Ephesian women had a problem along these lines (2 Tim. 3:5–7). Rather than making a ruling for all time, Paul was saying, "I am not *now* allowing a woman to teach" (this is also an accurate translation of the Greek text). He points out that Eve *became* a transgressor; that is, she was not created inferior (as was commonly believed then). His "let them learn" could have been a plea that women be taken seriously and allowed to learn correct doctrine (teaching women was considered a waste of time among both Greeks and Jews of that day). According to literature of the time, to "learn in quietness" was a mark of good breeding, so Paul would have wanted women to refrain from teaching until they had learned the basics.

But all of these are interpretive *possibilities*. The important thing is that this passage not be skimmed over so quickly that its difficulty is minimized and its "first impression" meaning used to overturn the clear teaching of other Scripture. Certainly it should never be used as some sort of restrictive instrument to shrink the service of female believers for all time.

Interpret a passage according to the best use of the original language. When I was a student at Los Angeles Baptist College, we who knew little about Greek still prided ourselves in finding out "what the Greek meant" in any Bible study we had. Sometimes pastors too will throw around their knowledge of Greek or Hebrew as though it makes them a cut above those in the pew.

Undoubtedly it helps to know the original languages, but even then one's presuppositions can cause a forced use that obscures or distorts the meaning of the text. Bible translators do not have as easy a time at their job as it would seem to the casual observer. Some *interpretation* is often necessarily mixed in with their *translation*. As one man has said, if the same word can mean "he kissed her" or "he spit on her" it makes a real difference which meaning is intended. But then, of course, it could be some of both.

Because of my work on a previous book, I am most familiar with errors in translation occuring because of translators' presuppositions regarding the restriction of women.[2] There is a good example of this type of problem in the way translators have often dealt with Romans 16:1–2 where Phoebe is called "servant" and "helper" or similar words in most translations. Unfortunately, the original language is not accurately translated by those words. The word "servant" (KJV) in verse 1 translates the Greek word *diakonos*. This Greek word appears twenty two times in Paul's writing, and in every other passage translators accurately render it "minister" or its transliteration "deacon." Only in the case of Phoebe is it translated "servant." In verse 2 the word "helper" (KJV) translates the Greek word *prostatis*. This word actually means "one who presides," "the chief of a party," and is used in the sense of leadership in its verb form elsewhere in the New Testament. Here it is translated in noun form, the only such occurence in the New Testament.

Probably these words describing Phoebe's position in the church were not accurately translated because the translators believed women were not allowed to hold such positions in the early church, so they said in effect, "It must mean something less." Their personal bias colored their translation work.

You can see by this example that it is important to have access to accurate information on the original language when interpreting Bible passages. In the case of Scripture about marriage, some passages have been neglected for such a long time by interpreters that the use of language is an essential area for us to investigate.

Interpret social teaching in line with doctrinal teaching. If we are all priests and kings before God (the doctrine of the priesthood of the believer 1 Peter 2:5, 9; Rev. 1:6; 5:10) and adopted sons (Gal. 4:4–7), it is not reasonable to ignore those equalizing positions and insist on a social practice (for example, segregation by race) that teaches by its example that some of us are better or more important than others.

Apply principles in a passage in harmony with their original use: It is possible to apply a Bible passage in such a way as to deny the very principle taught in it by insisting on copying precisely the behavior described or encouraged without determining first what the actual principle is. For example, insisting that women wear hats in church (because 1 Corinthians 11:5ff. says that women should wear head coverings while praying or prophesying) can defeat the principle taught in the Corinthians passage. The principle in this passage is that women should behave in a socially acceptable manner, so as not to bring disrepute to the gospel. Insisting women wear hats to church in an area where women do not wear hats as a requirement for respectable appearance would serve no good purpose. In fact, it could look rather foolish. Rather than an evidence of respectability, it would display inappropriateness and preoccupation with trivialities.

These are just some of the principles used in the study called hermeneutics. You can see that they are reasonable tools used to determine the most accurate and likely meaning of any portion of the Bible.

Marriage Customs

In order to understand many of the New Testament passages that refer to marriage, we must have some knowledge of what marriage was like in the first century among the Jewish community and in Greece and Rome. If we know about the lives of the recipients of the original Bible letters and the types of relationships they had with their marriage partners, it will not only be easier for us to see what God was trying to tell them, but also what He would tell us. So let's take a look at marriage first-century style.

Jewish Marriage

It is a bit difficult to pin down precise customs among Jewish people throughout the East at the time the New Testament was written because the Talmud, which gave the "oral law" or, as Jesus called it, "the traditions of men," really was oral at that time. It was passed down from teacher or "rabbi" to pupil. This body of material was not written down until well after the New Testament era. It does contain rules and rabbinic opinions about marriage that reflect practice at the time the New Testament events were taking place, but we cannot be certain to what *degree* these customs were practiced at the time.

However, we do know that the Jews held marriage in high regard, and that they thought everyone should be married. Old Testament writings reveal the Jewish joy in marriage.

There were laws in the Old Testament to protect women; these had been diluted and made ineffective by the teachings of the rabbinate. That is why it was so easy for a man to divorce his wife, "for any cause," as Jesus said. A husband could divorce his wife for burning the dinner, for going outdoors with her head uncovered, for speaking negatively about his parents, or even if he saw a prettier women he wanted to marry. But women could not divorce their husbands, and they had to leave their children with the ex-husband when they left his household.

Betrothals were contracted between consenting parties but were arranged by parents or others. A man was supposed to see his proposed wife at least once before the marriage in case he just couldn't stand the sight of her. A small coin was exchanged to seal the betrothal, perhaps a carry-over from the days of bride purchase, and a wedding document was drawn up stating the amount of money or property a woman was bringing to the marriage. Any other provisions to be agreed upon were included. Theoretically, this contract protected a wife from being cast out of her marriage penniless, but she was not really secure. Her husband had the right to keep the income from her dowry investments while they were married, and if she offended him by going out without her head covered or by committing any one of several other minor offenses (at least they seem so to us) she could be divorced without having her dowry returned to her at all.

A man was obligated to support his wife, and he had to ransom her if she were to be kidnapped. He also had to provide for her sexually by having intercourse with her regularly. This was not only for her sexual satisfaction, but to give her the children all Jewish women felt they had a right to. If a woman did not have children, it was a great shame to her.

The relationship between marriage partners was obviously an unequal one. Though love undoubtedly developed in many cases, it was not necessarily present. Women were considered inferior to men as evidenced in the prayer Jewish men recited, thanking God that they were not women. Women were considered unreliable witnesses, and their testimony was not admissible in legal matters. A rabbi would not even speak to his own wife in public.

Women had been exempted from many religious obligations under the law. The reason for this is now believed to be the need for mothers to be free to stay at home and care for their young children. But in New Testament times Jewish women simply were not seen as persons with special needs but as inferior persons. In the synagogue women were to be quiet out of respect for the congregation (the male members).

Not only were women considered to be inferior in status, but they were also believed to be inferior morally by nature.

The reason it was such a serious offense for a woman to go out with her head uncovered was that a woman, considered to be naturally sexually seductive, might seduce righteous men just by allowing them to see her hair. An extremely pious woman would not even uncover her hair in her own home except in the dark.

Greek Marriage

Middle and upper-class Greeks believed marriage to be a necessity in order to provide legitimate heirs to property but not particularly satisfying otherwise. As Menander said, "Marrying, to tell the truth, is an evil, but a necessary evil."[3]

Ideally women were to marry very young (around fourteen) while men were to be much older (thirty seven was the recommendation of one Greek writer). The reasoning behind this was that if a man could acquire his wife while she was young and impressionable, he could teach her how to manage his household the way he wanted it done. She would be easy to train and mold to fit his requirements.

The Greek man did not need a wife for companionship, love, or sexual fulfillment. It was socially acceptable for him to go to his own companions and paid entertainers for those things. Eroticism was part of Greek life to such an extent that it was not even considered immoral for the husband to have sexual relations with other women. However, there were severe penalties for an adulterous wife. And if a husband refused to repudiate his wife for her adultery, he also was punished. Adultery was seen more as a polluting of a man's right to a legitimate heir than as a violation of sexual trust. In some segments of Greek society there was no recognized crime of adultery, even for wives. This was for the simple reason that the Greeks felt it was impossible to prevent sexual contact when women (for example, merchant class or slave women) were allowed to move freely about in the company of men.

The Greek husband had legal responsibility for his wife's actions. Her legal position was much like that of a child or a slave: she went from the rule of her father to that of her husband. If her husband died, her son, if he was old enough, had legal authority over her and responsibility for her. If she had no qualifying son, she was given a male guardian to represent her.

Women from the upper and middle classes were kept at home in the women's quarters. These rooms were separate from the men's sleeping rooms, sometimes on a different floor. Wives worked at such things as spinning, weaving, and cooking; they also managed the household goods, kept the keys to the storerooms, directed the slaves, and oversaw the smooth operation of the home business of the family.

The upper and middle-class husband spent the majority of his time away from home where he was involved in his work, political activity, and evening entertainment. There was little common ground between husband and wife in Greek marriage. The wife was usually much younger, unschooled, and sheltered; the husband naturally found his companionship elsewhere.

Married Greeks in the merchant class worked together in the family business. (Priscilla and Aquila were tentmakers together.) Marriage between Greeks of this class must have involved much more day-to-day contact and comradeship.

There were also marriages between freed slaves and alliances between slaves and free men and women.

Roman Marriage

The Greek and Roman cultures were similar in that different classes of people contracted different types of marriage, and adultery with women who were slaves, merchants, or shopkeepers was nonpunishable because sexual contact with these women was seen as almost inevitable.

But there were also differences between the two cultures in the matter of marriage. In the Roman world, some types of marriage were more binding than others. In fact, the legal intricacies of what was marriage and what was not were so complicated that one wonders if even the Romans always knew whether they were legally married or not. Extensive dowries for wives sometimes gave them a larger part in the family finances than their husbands had, and Roman wives had more freedom to move about than did Greek wives. Many Roman women were well-educated. Some were even independently wealthy, owning large amounts of land.

> But emancipation entailed great danger for the civic and patrician woman. Not that a whole burden of responsibilities would fall on her, or that she would have to prove herself in profession and in public life to be the equal of man. On the contrary; boredom, leisure and wealth came to mold her character, and even the most careful education was not enough to help the girl come to

grips with her actual social helplessness and inactivity. It is thus not surprising that the ancient standard of morals was turned on its head and excesses, including cruelty and crime, were to be numbered among the great lady's pastimes?[4]

Ancient Romans had been under the law of *patria potestas* which gave the Roman father and husband absolute power (even of life and death) over his family. It is not clear to what extent this law still applied to the Roman family at the time the New Testament was written. But power over the family was still clearly in the hands of the husband and father even though some wives, especially in the upper classes, were able to find ways around both the law and their husbands and do as they wished with both their money and their persons.

Marriage Similarities in These Three Cultures

Before we end this chapter, I want to mention two areas that especially relate to our study. The first is the secular and private nature of marriage throughout the Mediterranean area at that time, and the second is the prevailing view that women were inferior to men.

In my research about first century marriage I have repeatedly encountered statements to the effect that marriage was a private family affair. This held true for the Jews, Greeks, and Romans. Though there were religious overtones to the marriage customs of these peoples, they were actually rites performed by the families of the couple to ensure the blessing of the household gods or to transfer the allegiance of the woman from the household gods of her father's home to those of her husband's home. There were also appeals for special help from gods who were in charge of a particular function or area. But all of this was a matter of personal or family participation. A professional religious leader did not marry the couple, nor was there a specific religious ceremony. The rites were a mixture of secular custom and family transfer. Even for the Jews it was a family matter, not a religious one needing the services of a rabbi.

It is important for us to realize the secular and private

nature of marriage during the time when biblical instructions on marriage were given; marriage was a fact of life separate from the formal religious life of those people. Marriage was seen as a practical necessity contracted between families rather than a divine, eternal alliance needing the assistance of a priest or minister. Seen in this light, there is all the more reason to regard instructions in the Bible as practical instructions on how to live as Christians within the marriages already existent and likely to be contracted. We can see why God would give practical, down-to-earth information in this area rather than some kind of mystical order to follow to mirror a divine plan.

The other area I want to mention is the obvious attitude prevalent that women were inferior persons. It was not that they were thought to be *positionally* inferior; they were believed to be *actually* inferior to men. Undoubtedly the effects of the Fall had a part in the oppression of women down through history just as it has contributed toward the oppression of other groups of people. Those who have power tend to oppress those beneath them in the hierarchical ladder. But there is a further reason that will help us see the ancient attitude toward women in a more realistic and maybe even a kinder light.

In the ancient world procreation was viewed in a decidedly unscientific manner. Those people knew nothing of sperm and ova, so they drew their own conclusions. Plants grew from seeds. Seeds grew in fertile fields. Therefore, the seed planted in woman by man grew into a child. This simple explanation was so universally accepted as the truth that if someone had posed the idea that the woman and the man both contributed to the child's origin, that person would have been labeled a fool. As David and Vera Mace state in *Marriage: East and West:*

> To the Eastern mind, therefore, the difference between the man and the woman was a basic difference, a fundamental difference of function. The woman could never be as important as the man, any more than the soil could be as important as the seed. By her very nature she was secondary, auxiliary. This is the very root of all the discrimina-

tion between man and woman that has characterized the history of the East, and in earlier times, of the West as well.[5]

Women were then, as they are even now in some places, considered to be the husband's fertile field. He sowed the seed; she grew it. This explains why it was acceptable and just in their eyes to send a mother away without her children in the case of divorce. After all, the children were products of the father. The mother merely nourished them to birth.

This attitude toward procreation also explains why women were often treated so much more harshly than men in matters of sexual offense. If only the man was responsible for the origin of the child, it was absolutely necessary for him to keep his wife from conceiving and producing some other man's child and foisting it off as heir to his property. The man, however, could be generous with his procreative powers, spreading his children around as contributions from himself to whoever would nourish them.

The men and women who first received New Testament instructions on marriage were already caught up in the results of these ancient beliefs about women. Rather than trying to correct their views on biology, God sent them instructions about marriage. The New Testament presented a way for husbands and wives to relate to each other (as equal persons) that could nullify the effects of prejudicial views about women.

But let's begin at the beginning. God was at work to equalize marriage long before New Testament times. Let's take a look at the first marriage.

---

1. For a more extensive study of this passage see my book *Woman Be Free*, Zondervan, 1977, Chapter 5.

2. Ibid.

3. Verena Zinserling, *Women in Greece and Rome* (New York: Abner Schram, 1973), p. 26.

4. Ibid., p. 55.

5. David and Vera Mace, *Marriage: East and West* (Garden City: Dophin Books, 1960), pp. 30-31.

HEIRS TOGETHER

6

The First Marriage

The first marriage took place without courtship, ceremony, or vows. Adam and Eve saw each other, and they *knew*. I suppose this is the only case of love at first sight that wasn't criticized by an observer.

This first couple undoubtedly realized they had a unique relationship. They knew they were not like the animals, and they also knew they were not exactly like God. They were "man in fellowship" as Paul Jewett so aptly puts it. Sexuality as expressed in an act would be a natural and eventual result, but would not by any means be all or even the main part of that fellowship. They saw each other as "someone like me" and rejoiced in the recognition.

What were their positions in this first human relationship? Was the man the leader? Or the woman? Or were they equals? There is a school of thought that contends that the most ancient human societies were matriarchal in nature. Those who hold this view would probably opt for woman as the leader. Then there are those who think man has always led the woman because of a created order between the sexes existing from the beginning. But I am going to opt for what I believe has the best biblical evidence to support it. I think Adam and Eve were equals and shared whatever decisions they needed to make.

The First Creation Account: Genesis 1:26–28

Then God said, "Let us make man in our image, in our likeness, and let them rule over the fish of the sea and the birds of the air, over the livestock, over all the earth, and over all the creatures that move along the ground."
So God created man in his own image,
in the image of God he created him;
male and female he created them.
God blessed them and said to them, "Be fruitful and increase in number; fill the earth and subdue it. Rule over the fish of the sea and the birds of the air and over every creature that moves on the ground.

This first account of human creation is presented as one event, with male and female created together as "man" in God's image. They were given co-regency over all the earth. There was no differentiation of power or position, no order or hierarchy established here. Further, God declared in the verses following this account that all He had created was "good."

The Second Creation Account: Genesis 2:7, 20–24

And the Lord God formed man from the dust of the ground and breathed into his nostrils the breath of life, and man became a living being.
So the man gave names to all the livestock, the birds of the air and all the beasts of the field.
But for Adam no suitable helper was found. So the Lord God caused the man to fall into a deep sleep; and while he was sleeping, he took one of the man's ribs and closed up the place with flesh. Then the Lord God made a woman from the rib he had taken out of the man, and he brought her to the man. The man said,
"This is now bone of my bones
and flesh of my flesh;
she shall be called 'woman,'
for she was taken out of man."

> For this reason a man will leave his father and mother and
> be united with his wife, and they will become one flesh.

According to some, the last part of this passage contains one of the indications of early matriarchy. They claim that if the man had been the dominant partner, the woman would have been expected to leave her father and mother to go with her husband instead of his leaving his parents to go with her. And the first part of this passage is used by those who insist on male dominance to prove that woman is by God's design fitted for an auxiliary relationship with man but not an equal one. They cite the word "helper" or, more usually, the King James Version's "help meet," as proof of woman's subordinate position. I'll still opt for the relationship of equality from the biblical evidence. Let's look more closely at those words "suitable helper" and "help meet."

Helpmeet or Ezer and Neged?

In modern Christian circles wives are usually referred to as helpmeets (or helpmates) to their husbands. The term combines two King James Version words used to translate the Hebrew words *ezer* and *neged,* and we now think of "helpmeet" as modern English usage. To us a helper is someone who is an assistant, lower in status and job description than the one helped. The cumulative impression is that a helpmeet is kind of a glorified gal Friday. But the original language does not carry any such meaning for these words.

Ezer, the word translated "help" or "helper," occurs repeatedly in the Old Testament. Elsewhere it never refers to a subordinate helper; instead, it is used to identify an equal help or one with superior power. The word is often used in reference to God as our helper as in Psalm 121:1–2:

> I lift up my eyes to the hills—
>   where does my help come from?
> My help comes from the Lord,
>   the Maker of heaven and earth.

Neged, the word translated as "meet" or "suitable," is a preposition in Hebrew, but to translate it as a preposition in

English would obscure its meaning. It is used elsewhere to mean "corresponding to" or "fit for."

The combined sense of the two words *ezer* and *neged* is that Eve was an appropriate, fitting partner for Adam. Rather than being proof of a subordinate position for Eve, these words, according to the best use of the original language, support her position as Adam's equal. She was not only his equal, but was his equal in a positive way. She would be a *real help*! She was *like* Adam, suitable in every way. He recognized this immediately as he exclaimed, "Ah, at last! Bone of my bone and flesh of my flesh."

Rather than teaching a subordinate-superior hierarchical relationship for man and woman, this passage presents a relationship of mutuality. It may also be God's way of showing that women were to be regarded as fully human by future generations of His people, not disdained and degraded as they have been throughout the world.

Getting the Right One

When Adam and Eve first knew each other, everything was new and untainted. There was none of the misery and trouble that came after the Fall to strain their relationship. They saw each other as equals and as delightful. That was the first marriage.

They probably got along perfectly well without ever a disagreement, stalemate, or difficulty, right? Wrong. Even the most perfect match in the history of the world, the participants chosen by God, deteriorated into the Fall. The woman and man both made excuses for their disobedience, the man even blaming God for "this woman you gave me."

I mention this here because when we are disgusted with our husband or wife we are all prone to think that maybe, just *maybe* we got the wrong one, that some other man or woman would have been easier to live with. I know I have thought that. And one day when I was thinking just that, my mind fastened on a startling bit of information: *If getting the exactly right marriage partner is the key to success, then Adam and Eve had the ideal potential for a perfect marriage. But they disobeyed God together, blamed each other for their disobedience, and even denounced each other.* Then the marriage of Rebekah and Isaac came to mind. If ever there was care taken in trying to get a guaranteed good match with God's direction, this was it. Abraham sent his chief servant all the way back to Mesopotamia to find a wife for his son. The servant prayed for divine guidance, and the girl was found. High hopes for the marriage abounded. But if we look at this marriage years later, we see deception, favoritism in both parents for "their" child, and tragedy as a result.

Adam and Eve had perfect potential. But together they lost their home in Eden and produced a son who killed his brother. Their own daily choices determined what their lives were like, not the perfection of the original match. Isaac and Rebekah let their relationship deteriorate, dragging their sons down also. God doesn't seem to hand out perfect marriage partners or guarantees of harmony based upon the choice of a mate.

Someone once said that being the best marriage partner was more important than finding one. I thought at the time, that sounds nice but rather unrealistic. What if you marry someone who is really terrible? And I will concede that there are unions that are so unworkable and miserable it seems they cannot be mended even though one of the partners is doing his or her absolute best to be the right kind of marriage partner. It takes more than one to make a successful partnership. But the principle is still sound. It is what you do with what you have that counts, rather than wishing you had found Prince or Princess Charming before you married a frog by mistake.

Effects of the Fall

Your desire will be for your husband
and he will rule over you (Gen. 3:16).

Over the centuries these words have been used to support the imposing of the medieval Order of Things on the marriage relationship. This verse is an important link in the chain-of-command philosophy and has long been interpreted as God's decree that woman, whatever her relationship to man previous to the Fall, is thereafter to be in subjection to man. Some have said it means that all women are to be in subjection to all men. Others say this only applies to the marriage relationship—that to maintain an orderly and peaceful home, someone must be in authority, and this verse gives that authority to man in perpetuity.

But do these interpretations hold up under the scrutiny of good interpretive principles? Or do these interpretations reflect Bible study methods that are more like the medieval Bible study methods than the methods now accepted as more accurate and revealing of the real meaning of the Scriptures?

To interpret this verse as restricting the woman's participation in marriage to being follower and submitter, forcing the man to be leader and authoritarian, one must tear it away from its surroundings. To maintain the hierarchical interpretation one must ignore the context.

When looking at the passage as a whole *within* its context, the issue becomes: is this information a *decree* from God or is it a *prediction*? Is God telling this human couple that from now on this is the way it *must* be? Or is He telling our first parents that this is the way the world will go now that sin has entered into it? Is it a curse decreed upon them or a natural result of their actions? For if it is a decreed curse, there is no escape from it. It *must* be. But if it is a prediction, then there is an alternative. There is room for grace to change the results of sin.

It is ironic that we have no difficulty at all seeing that the references to the man and the soil and death are predictions. Those effects are not seen as unchangeable decrees representative of what God wants for us. In fact, we work to ameliorate and modify them. We try to make toil less burdensome for man, and we work to help the ground bring forth things other than thorns and thistles. Even much of what we do as service to God serves to frustrate the sentence of death; we prolong life and assuage pain whenever we can. But somehow woman is exempted from our interpretation of the rest of this passage.

We are told that she must be under man's dominion "because Genesis 3:16 says so." Women even write such things about themselves: "I know it is God's will for me because the Bible says my nature has been changed so that I need a man to rule over me."

But the language here is predictive; the Hebrew construction is a form generally used in a predictive sense. And there is no indication from the context that it should be used in any other way. Thus, it is reasonable to interpret the passage as predictive, as prophecy not penalty—as God saying, in effect, this is the way the world will go.

If we interpret this section as an unfailing decree, then we cannot single woman out, for that is poor interpretive practice. We must give the same weight to the decree about thorns and thistles and not try to thwart them. And we must certainly insist that man work by the sweat of his brow till he die. That means no more retirement, fellows, and toss out your antiperspirants too.

To take the statements connected with the Fall (in Genesis 3) as other than predictions would result in actions that are everything from heartless to absurd. Unfortunately, the church has at times insisted on interpreting them in just such a way. Painkillers have been denied to those needing them, especially for the pain of difficult childbirth because of a misinterpretation of the first half of Genesis 3:16. And many still cling to the medieval interpretation concerning husband and wife relationships.

"Worldliness" Begins

But what does this passage mean? *Your desire will be for your husband, and he will rule over you.*

I believe it means the woman will more and more tend to rely upon her husband, be dependent upon him because of her many pregnancies and small children to care for, and as a result of her dependency, he will take advantage of her need and dominate her. I think it predicts the beginning of the true essence of worldliness: Those who are vulnerable look to the powerful for help, and the powerful exploit their power and rule over and mistreat the vulnerable. The process becomes complex and intertwined, extending itself geometrically until it has permeated all relationships and affected all people. While the weak turn to the strong, they resent their own vulnerability and the oppression it will bring them; thus, the weak maneuver and manipulate and misuse the strong when they discover the weaknesses *they* have. On the one side there is the groveling slave who works only when the master is watching and wastes his goods; on the other, there is the rich landowner who keeps his tenants in poverty while he lives in splendor. There is the husband who denies his wife what she wants just because he can, while the wife humiliates him and gossips about him in return. It is a never-ending circle of exploitation and retaliation.

Fortunately, this circle of worldliness caused by the Fall can be broken by Christ's provision. Salvation restores our fellowship with God. The Holy Spirit not only gives us back the lost access to God, but also enables us to know how to reunite ourselves with each other again as equals, mending that interpersonal break as well. And it is this banner of freedom in Christ and the equality of believers that carries us on toward reversing the principles of worldliness which teach us to exploit and manipulate; we can go on to relationships of non-exploitation and non-manipulation in which each person is of equal value with equal opportunity to experience and express his or her full personhood.

In the past, we have taken this prediction of sin's result and have tried to institutionalize it and enforce it as God's will for us. Instead, we should be working to reverse it (as we have the other results of the Fall) and reinstate that lost relationship of mutual responsibility and respect that was present before the Fall. God provided a Savior to mend the broken relationship between His human creation and Himself. Now He wants to work through us, His creation, to reverse the bad effects of the Fall. It is time we worked with Him to reinstate the original relationship between man and woman in marriage.

Advantages in the First Marriage

Even though Adam and Eve had to experience the anguish of remembering their lost paradise after the Fall, they had some advantages over us in their marriage.

There were only two of them, and they were the first people to be married. There was no one else around to tell them how they should relate to each other or what roles they should try to mold themselves into. There weren't even any in-laws. Of course that meant no baby-sitters either, so I guess it wasn't all gravy. But then, where did they have to go?

The point is, Adam and Eve could make this marriage any way they wanted it to be. They could be themselves, work out their differences without interference or preconceived ideas about which one should take out the garbage. They could decide on each issue as it arose.

Suppose you and your mate could go to the proverbial desert island. And suppose that you would not need anyone for medical help or any other reason, so you could safely stay as long as you liked. Couldn't you two get along pretty well there? You would have to work things out or be very lonely.

Why not live *as if*. Why not live as if you can, between the two of you, decide how you want to live, what you want to do, how you want to divide work and responsibilities? Why not live as if there were no other people to interfere, no preconceived ideas about what you should do? Why not?

It is your marriage. You aren't married to your parents, so you don't have to live like them. You aren't married to your neighbors, or your teachers, or your friends. You are married to each other. Why not act like it?

We cannot go back to the Garden of Eden to reclaim that original privacy, but we can create a privacy and codetermination of our own to a degree far greater than most of us have imagined. We can stop trying to dominate each other or to live by formula. We can, bit by bit, rebuild our marriage relationship into one that is really ours, not leftovers from everybody else's marriages. The principle of mutual submission can help, and we will look at that in the next chapter.

HEIRS
HEIRS
HEIRS
HEIRS
HEIRS
TOGETHER

7

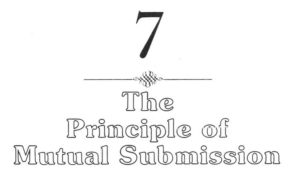

7

The
Principle of
Mutual Submission

What do I mean when I say the principle most helpful and necessary in marriage is that of *mutual submission?* Do I mean he tells her what to do and she tells him what to do? A trade-off in domination? No, I don't. I knew a couple who had a marriage like that. He bossed her around and controlled her actions. She couldn't do things that he didn't like or that he thought were unladylike or "unspiritual." So she lived a cramped life and was a bit neurotic. He, on the other hand, was controlled by her in a different way. He submitted to her emotionally—not willingly, I think, but they had this trade-off situation as though they had a silent agreement to make each other miserable. *He* was always in hot water for making her sad or nervous, or for offending someone (in her opinion). And *she* was always in fear of doing something that would disobey his commands. That's *not* the kind of mutual submission I have in mind!

I'm talking about mutual submission as reflected in several New Testament passages and in some Old Testament happenings. It is, surprisingly, the kind of relationship Sarah and Abraham must have had at least some of the time, as we will see later when we examine 1 Peter 3. I think it is presented most clearly in Ephesians 5:21: "Submitting yourselves one to another in the fear of God" (KJV).

Mutual submission is a way of living, an attitude toward others. It is something one does because one wants to, not because one has to. This Ephesians passage really begins with verse 18 of Ephesians 5. Paul has been talking about, among other things, the contrasts between the old way (pagan) and the new way of living (in Christ). In verse 18 he begins with a command, "Be not drunk with wine (which was not just a part of a wine-drinking culture, but a part of the pagan Greek religious practice) . . . , but (the contrast) be filled with the Spirit." Then follows in the original language a series of participles telling the believer in which areas they are to be filled with the Spirit—a working out of this new way in Christ. These participles are: *giving* thanks, *speaking* to yourselves in psalms and hymns, and *submitting* yourselves one to another. This was the Spirit-filled way, in contrast to the pagan way that naturally resulted from pagan worship. They drank wine, and in drunkenness and emotional frenzy they thanked their gods, sang, and related to one another.

In our study of relationships between Christians, verse 21 steps out to meet us with this curious gentle suggestion on how we can relate to each other in a "filled-with-the-Spirit" way—by submitting ourselves to one another in the fear of God.

I can almost hear the Ephesians saying, "How in the world can we do that with our relationships set up as they are?" Paul must have anticipated their difficulty because he then tells them how. The several verses following 21 tell the believers how they can work out this mutual submitting in their own very rigid hierarchical social system. How would a slave live out this attitude of mutual submission with his master (who owns his body)? And how would the master submit to his slave? Paul tells them both.

The different social strata in Greek life were so unequal in power that for Paul to have given them instructions to submit without explaining how to work this out in their own situations would have caused all manner of abuses of the principle. Can't you just hear slaves saying, "Now that I am a Christian and you, Master, are too, we should submit to each other. So you do my work today, and I will do yours!" You can take it from there with children and fathers, husbands and wives. These verses were given to those people because they needed to know how to live out this new way, how to love each other without exploiting each other.

Mutual submission was a *principle* given to guide relationships between *all* believers. The verses following verse 21 tell how to work it out in three of the most unequal relationships in the society of that day. Paul begins with the relationship between wives and husbands.

Paul's instruction to wives has often been misunderstood and misinterpreted in the past. Part of the reason is that English translations of verse 22 have usually begun the verse with a command, "Wives submit," and have made no connection at all between verses 22 and 21. But they cannot be separated, for in the original language they are a continuous sentence with verse 22 having no participle of its own. The word so often translated "submit" does not occur in the text of 22, and it is inaccurate to use it. The participle in 22 is the *participle understood* from the previous verse. In the Greek text it reads: "Submitting yourselves to one another in the fear of Christ, wives to your own husbands as to the Lord in everything." The participle is *hupotassomenoi*, in the middle voice. Used thus, it is not a command to wives to submit, but is a call to self volitional submission by all believers. The following words to wives tell them *how* to work this out, *how* to submit in relation to their husbands. Wives are to submit to husbands *as to the Lord* and *in everything*. A lack of attention to the original language and a lack of knowledge of first-century Greek married life has caused this passage to be misunderstood.

You recall that Greek wives and husbands did not usually

have the close contact or companionship we experience in modern Western marriages. They were not necessarily even friends. And the Greek wife was already submitted. There was no point in commanding her to submit to her husband; she had to, legally and practically. She really didn't have any choice in the matter. But there was a need to tell her how to submit in a Christian manner. Her attitude toward her husband now was to be one of respect and honor "as to the Lord." And it was to be "in everything," not only when he was looking or might find out about it later. This instruction speaks directly to the Greek wife's position as underling. It was so tempting to get back at an all-powerful husband for his neglect and mistreatment. A woman could waste and spoil her husband's goods, talk disparagingly about him, and be generally disrespectful and divisive. She could also shame him publicly and cause trouble for him by behaving in a disreputable or illegal manner. Oh, there were lots of things she could do to even the score. But the Christian woman was to stop all this destructive behavior.

Following the words to the wife, the husband is instructed, for his part in this mutual submission, to love his wife as himself. This part of the passage also is often misunderstood because it is not seen in relation to verse 21. Frequently it is presented as an almost impossible goal for a man. He is encouraged to have a kind of holy, mystical, superior love for his wife that can somehow raise her to a higher spiritual level. That is not what Paul is instructing at all. He is talking about a simple, practical outworking of mutual submission that hit the Greek husband precisely where he needed it. Power corrupts, and absolute power corrupts absolutely, as the saying goes. The Greek husband had nearly absolute power over his wife. And he erred in precisely this area—the misuse of superior power by degrading and misusing his wife. So Paul tells the husband to treat his wife with *the same kind of consideration with which he treats himself.* This raises her to the same level with him. And she, by treating him with the respectful and honorable manner she holds for Christ, stops the undercutting destructive ways of the manipulating underdog. Thus, in this rigidly patriarchal culture, it was possible to have a relationship of equals. They became equal *persons, to each other.* They were living lives of mutual submission.

From this passage, and others that reflect it (1 Cor. 7:3–4; 1 Cor. 11:11–12; Gal. 3:28; Col. 3:11; Luke 22:25–27), the principle of mutual submission shines forth. It is not just a principle for husbands and wives but for all relationships between all believers. In every walk of life, and in every station, we are persons of equal value and should treat each other accordingly.

The rest of this passage goes on to tell the Ephesian believers how to work out mutual submission in two other very unequal relationships, those of father and child, and master and slave. Their situations were similar to those of husband and wife, in that one member had all the legal rights and power along with the temptations to lord it over the other that go with such power. The other member in each twosome held the position of legal and social underdog with all the temptations that went with it to maneuver, manipulate, and get even with the "overdog."

This long passage carries a message about power and the misuse of it by both sides, and it ends with that in mind: "In conclusion, be strong in the Lord and in the strength of His might" (Eph. 6:10 MLB). Believers are to use power as the Lord would use it, not to oppress but to serve each other kindly. Again, the contrast is shown between the old way they had lived in paganism where their gods were more oppressive and selfish than humans, and the new way in Christ in which love motivated service and non-exploitation. "I call you my friends," Jesus had said, and they were to be that to each other too, on every level.

What is mutual submission? It is not self-negation and letting yourself be a doormat. It is saying, in effect, "You are as valuable as I am, and so I will not take advantage of you. By the same token, I am as valuable as you are, so you should not take advantage of me either."

But doesn't this lead to hair-splitting and a legalistic view of one's relationship? You know, the old 50-50 dilemma? I suppose it could, if it were not for the Person who began this whole passage in Ephesians 5:18 and to whom we all have access. Verse 18 says, "Be filled with the Spirit." And it is the Holy Spirit who can show us, as individuals and collectively, how to work out our own situations according to this principle.

We do not need rigid rules. We have the biblical principle—mutual submission. And we have the Holy Spirit to help us put it into practice and to lead us in all the variations of our lives and marriages. He is always there.

HEIRS HEIRS HEIRS HEIRS HEIRS HEIRS

TOGETHER

8

8

Headship – What Is It?

A wife with strength of character is a crown to her husband (Prov. 12:4 MLB).

I thought it would be easy to define *head* in English. That was before I looked it up in the dictionary. *Head* takes up at least a half page in my large dictionary, while another whole page is devoted to words with *head* as a prefix, such as *headache, head-man,* and *head-on,* which is how I intended to approach the subject. I thought I would simply look at the English usage of the word *head* to find out why we see headship as leadership in marriage. But the dictionary gives so many meanings for *head* that "leader" comes about fourteenth on the list.

However, I found *headship* itself as a separate entry. So the dictionary does have a description for the title: "The position or authority of a chief, or leader; leadership; command."

The next question then becomes: What is the biblical definition of headship? Do the American English definitions and the biblical descriptions match? And if they don't, which one do you want to choose to follow?

Actually, the word *headship* isn't in the Bible as such. Scripture talks about someone being the head of something or someone, but never about a headship concept. That is an invention of our own, or of someone who came before us.

Let's look at some uses of the word *head* in the New Testament that might have some bearing on the subject.

> Instead, speaking the truth in love, we will in all things grow up into him who is the Head, that is, Christ. From him the whole body, joined and held together by every supporting ligament, grows and builds itself up in love, as each part does its work (Eph. 4:15–16).

Here Christ is presented as both the source of our maturing in the Christian life and of the power for harmonious living together in the body of believers.

> He is before all things, and in him all things hold together. And he is the head of the body, the church; he is the beginning and the firstborn from among the dead, so that in everything he might have the supremacy (Col. 1:17–18).

Christ is seen again as the origin and source for all life and for the life of the church in particular. And again He as head has a unifying effect on His body, the body of believers.

> Do not let anyone who delights in false humility and the worship of angels disqualify you for the prize. Such a person goes into great detail about what he has seen, and his unspiritual mind puffs him up with idle notions. He has lost connection with the Head, from whom the whole body, supported and held together by its ligaments and sinews, grows as God causes it to grow (Col. 2:18–19).

Again Christ is the source of nourishment and harmony and is the believer's means of discernment.

> (Christ is seated) far above all rule and authority, power and dominion, and every title that can be given, not only in the present age but also in the one to come. And God placed all things under his feet and appointed him to be head over everything for the church, which is his body,

the fullness of him who fills everything in every way (Eph. 1:21–22).

Jesus' position is "far above all rule and authority, power and dominion" and it is *for* the church not *over* the church. His church is raised up to sit beside Him and share all this: "And God raised us up with Christ and seated us with him in the heavenly realms in Christ Jesus" (Eph. 2:6).

In all these examples Christ is a loving, serving, uniting, nourishing, sharing Savior. Authoritarian rule over the church is not the message here at all. Instead, as head He personifies His own instructions to His disciples in the following verses.

Jesus called them together and said, "You know that the rulers of the Gentiles lord it over them and their high officials exercise authority over them. Not so with you. Instead, whoever wants to become great among you must be your servant, and whoever wants to be first must be your slave—just as the Son of Man did not come to be served, but to serve, and to give his life as a ransom for many" (Matt. 20:25–28).

In the New Testament there are other uses of the word *head.* In Matthew 5:36 Jesus tells His listeners not to swear by their heads, and in Luke 7:46 He reprimands His Pharisee host for not anointing His head with oil. In both cases the head is representative of the honor of the invididual. Throughout the East, then as now, a person's head was the seat of personal honor and respect. To be insulting toward someone's head was and is the greatest dishonor and insult.

Now that we have looked at several New Testament usages of *head* as referring to the physical body's most honorable part and as Christ is presented as "head" of the church, His body, let's look at the Scripture passages referring to marriage which use the word *head* in reference to the husband.

1 Corinthians 11:3–12

Now I want you to realize that the head of every man is Christ, and the head of the woman is man, and the head of Christ is God. Every man who prays or prophesies with

his head covered dishonors his head. And every woman
who prays or prophesies with her head uncovered dishonors her head—it is just as though her head were
shaved. If a woman does not cover her head, she should
have her hair cut off, and if it is a disgrace for a woman to
have her hair cut or shaved off she should cover her head.
A man ought not to cover his head, since he is the image
and glory of God; but the woman is the glory of man. For
man did not come from woman, but woman from man;
neither was man created for woman, but woman for man.
For this reason, and because of the angels, the woman
ought to have a sign of authority on her head.

In the Lord, however, woman is not independent of
man, nor is man independent of woman. For as woman
came from man, so also man is born of woman. But everything comes from God.

The first thing we notice in looking at the use of *head* in
this passage is that it is not used as it was in the passages in
which Christ is presented as the head of the church, nor is it
like the usage in Ephesians 1 where Christ is seen as far above
all principalities, authority, and earthly power. It does not talk
about nourishing and growing toward the head one has, nor
does it talk about Christ as head of all believers. Instead, there
is a complex interweaving of several meanings for the word
head. It is used figuratively (as in the first sentence) and literally (covering and uncovering or shaving the head) and culturally (shameful and disgraceful to have heads covered or uncovered).

Figurative Use of the Word Head

How was God the head of Christ, Christ the head of the
man, and the man the head of the woman? If we look at this
passage in the light of Greek culture, we can understand this.
To the Greeks, the physical head was the seat of honor. One's
head represented one's honor. By behaving dishonorably, one
shamed one's own head. But the way one behaved also
reflected on the person responsible for one.

Head could have the figurative meaning of "origin" here.
Christ's origin was God. The man had his origin in Christ (the
Creator). And in that culture, the idea that new life originated

entirely in the male, that a mother was only the fertile field ripening the husband's child, would also place the male as origin of the female. To them, man was the source of woman in more ways than one. Therefore, figuratively *head* could refer to one's source and honor. Later in the passage we see that the concern Paul expresses is that a believer not dishonor one's head, either literally or figuratively. Christ could have (theoretically) dishonored His head, God, if He had behaved dishonorably. A man could dishonor Christ by behaving dishonorably. And a woman could dishonor a man (her husband) by behaving dishonorably—in this case, by not covering her head. We will see why later.

Literal Use of the Word Head

The physical head was regarded as something to be either covered or uncovered while praying or prophesying. Women were to cover their heads. Men were to uncover theirs. For a woman, an uncovered head was as bad as having short hair or a shaved head. Why this concern over heads covered or uncovered, shaven or unshaven? For the answer we must look at the context of the passage and at Greek and Jewish custom.

Context and Cultural Information

This passage is within a context of "doing things decently and in order." Paul was guiding the Corinthian believers out of the forest of their past way of life, helping them see which behavior was profitable and which was unprofitable even if not forbidden. He begins chapter 10 by telling them that even though the Israelites were all under the cloud and received God's provision, God was not pleased with all of them because of the behavior of some. The behavior of believers could thwart God's work. Beginning with verse 23 (chapter 10) he tells them, "Everything is permissible—but not everything is beneficial. Everything is permissible—but not everything is constructive." Then he deals with the subject of eating meat that had been sacrificed to idols. His point in the whole passage is that, free as we are as Christians from the false mean-

ings of pagan custom, we have to be careful what the effect will
be if we flaunt all custom. We must evaluate and choose wisely
in exercising our freedom. He begins chapter 11 with these
words, "Follow my example, as I follow the example of
Christ." He is not saying that we should take him, Paul, as our
perfect example in everything but that in this case, that of
doing what we do for the good of others, we should follow
Christ's example, as he does. Jesus did not do everything He
could do, but did what He did, even limiting His freedom at
times, for the good of others.

Paul then addresses the issue of head coverings as part of
the same subject. The Corinthians needed to know that not
adhering to certain proprieties could, by association, discredit
the gospel and cause others to be led astray. Even though a
Christian was not conscience-bound to the practice itself, since
the basis for it had no more hold over him now that he was free
in Christ, he or she must realize the consequences if the practice was disregarded.

What was the cultural significance of head covering? And
how would this affect the believer? Respectable Greek women
wore a distinctive head covering. Temple prostitutes and paid
entertainers (hetaerae) did not. So if a Greek woman were to
take off her head-dress, she would appear to be sexually
promiscuous.

For the Hellenic Jewish woman the headdress was also
important. Jews believed that a woman's hair was a sexual
enticement. Any woman seen outside her house with her hair
uncovered was automatically considered to be a loose woman,
even an adulteress. As I mentioned in another chapter, this is
why going out without a head covering was grounds for divorce and confiscation of a woman's dowry. Thus, it would be
disgraceful for a woman to leave off her headdress in the public meeting. To preserve the sense of propriety necessary to be
taken seriously and not being seen as unprincipled, licentious
cultists, Christians had to be careful not to arouse suspicions
about their morality among their pagan neighbors.

What about men uncovering their heads while praying

and prophesying? According to Dr. Lee Anna Starr the Greek male recognized the divinity of a god during worship by baring the head.[1] For a Christian man to pray or prophesy without uncovering his head would signify to the unbeliever that Christ was not truly God, a denial of His divinity. The man would thus dishonor Christ and his own head by worshiping in an improper manner.

If this passage is seen in the light of its context and the cultural situation of the time, it does not appear to award the husband a position of authority over his wife. It simply recognized the prevailing attitudes toward head coverings and instructs both men and women about their responsibilities for impressions they would make regarding honor and dishonor.

Verses 8–10 (chapter 11) seem at first glance to say that there is some kind of permanent hierarchy between woman and man, but in the verses immediately following Paul denies that this is the case for believers. He says, "In the Lord, however," and goes on to show the interdependence of man and woman, their equality in Christ, and their ultimate reliance on God.

There are several theories as to what verses 8–10 may mean.[2] The part about the angels is particularly puzzling and gives rise to far-out possibilities posed by a few commentators. Perhaps we do not have enough information about the situation at Corinth to know exactly why these verses are there. Paul may have been referring to a commonly held belief about the reason women were not to go without their head coverings to show the Corinthian believers how inappropriate it would be for them to do so. (At about that time, Jewish superstition held that women could be seduced by evil angels.) Paul may have been showing them that "in the Lord" this was not so, but the fact that it was so widely believed was reason enough for them to wear head coverings for the sake of decorum.

But what is the message here for us? As believers it is certainly true that we should be aware of what our actions say about us in the light of what is generally considered to be honorable behavior. We do not want to appear as thieves when we do not steal, or as liars when we are honest, or as profligate, when we are chaste.

What does it say to us that is applicable to marriage now? It says to me that I should not dishonor my husband by my actions. That if I find myself in a society in which certain actions will shame or humiliate him, I will refrain from them even though they are not wrong in themselves. The principle would be the same for husbands. In this society, we as married persons represent one another by association. We should do nothing to discredit or diminish the self-respect or reputation of the other. We should be good representatives of the partnership.

Ephesians 5:23

For the husband is the head of the wife as Christ is the head of the church, his body, of which he is the Savior.

This verse tells in what way the husband is the head of his wife. It is as Christ is the head of the church. And it says that Christ is the head of the church in that He is the Savior of the body. This usage is similar to that in the verses quoted early in this chapter showing Christ in a nourishing, saving position, unifying His body, the church. Taken by itself the above verse would have a rather obvious application. The husband is to see himself as "savior of the wife's body," that is, as provider and protector, and that only. The idea of "head" as authority is not presented in this verse itself. But in verse 23 it does not occur by itself; it is preceded by a verse that says in most translations, "Wives, submit to your husbands as to the Lord," making verse 23 appear to be part of a command to wives.

Some of the following material may seen repetitious because Ephesians 5:21, 22 was explained in an earlier chapter. However, I am restating some of this information because it is necessary to the understanding of verse 23 which pertains to our study of the idea of headship.

Both husbands and wives have had problems knowing how to apply Ephesians 5:22 as it is usually translated. If it means wives are to submit in everything as they would to the Lord, then does that mean the husband is in the position of God? Does a wife have to do *everything* her husband tells her to do? Even if it is wrong? Some say yes. Others say she obeys and submits to everything that is not wrong. But then the problem is: Who decides what is wrong? And how wrong does it have to be before she can go against her husband's will? Any way you look at it, applying this verse presents problems if it is a command to wives to submit to husbands.

For if we believers are ultimately responsible only to God, does not such submission to a fallible husband put someone else between a woman and God? And is it right that a human husband should have such complete responsibility for the life of another mature adult who may be as capable, or even more capable, as he is to make decisions about her own life?

If we look at the whole passage within its larger context, examine the language carefully, and then consider some cultural factors, we find that the seeming command is not a command at all. It becomes neither puzzling nor difficult to apply to a marriage relationship.

The Context

There are several themes that recur throughout the Book of Ephesians. Paul repeatedly talks about love, freedom balanced by responsibility, and the goal of unity among believers. He also keeps contrasting the old pagan way with the new Christ way. In chapter 5, verses 1–2 he says, "Be imitators of God, therefore, as dearly loved children and live a life of love, just as Christ loved us and gave himself up for us as fragrant offerings and sacrifice to God."

In 5:18 he gives an imperative, a command: "Do not get drunk on wine. . . . Instead, be filled with the Spirit." This command, "Be filled with the Spirit" (the Christ way as opposed to the pagan way) is then followed by a series of participles in the original language. Some translations do not render this series of participles as such but turn them into commands, or turn some into commands and not others. They are:

"speaking to yourselves in psalms and hymns" (v. 19); "giving thanks" (v. 20); and "submitting to one another" (v. 21). The several verses following verse 21 address wives, husbands, children, fathers, servants (slaves), masters, and conclude with instructions about using power as Christ did (6:10).

The passage as a whole, within the larger context beginning with 5:18 and ending with 6:10, is about the use and misuse of power, the Christian way to unity (mutual submission of believers), and the contrast between the pagan way and the Christ way. Within the larger framework of the Book of Ephesians it reflects these themes also.

Language

I have already mentioned that the only command in the early portion of this passage is in 5:18 ("be filled with the Spirit"), and that the words following, usually translated as commands, are actually not imperatives but participles in the original language. This is particularly important for the subject we are studying now—that is, the marriage relationship—because in verse 21 ("submitting yourselves one to another in the fear of God," KJV) a volitional mutual submission is encouraged for all believers toward all other believers. This word "submitting" translates the Greek word *hupotassomenoi*. It is a voluntary "putting oneself under the other" applying to all.

This call to mutual submission was a way to Christian unity. With the Spirit's guidance and help believers were to award each other preferential treatment. This would be the great equalizer in a society of extreme inequality. But how could they apply it on a practical level? The following verses tell how.

The unseverable connection between this verse and those following it is evident by the absence of a participle (or verb) in verse 22. Verse 22, so often translated as a command for wives, must take its participle from the previous verse, for it has no verb or participle of its own. *Hupotassomenoi* becomes the participle *understood* in verse 22. Instead of beginning a new subject (husbands and wives), verse 22 continues the thought and meaning begun in verse 21. *Hupotassomenoi* cannot legitimately be translated as a command (wives submit) in verse 22 because it is not an imperative in verse 21. As an extension of the thought begun in verse 21, mutual submission of all believers, verse 22 is first in a series of instructions about how to work out this mutual submission of all believers in some particular situations.

Greek wives did not need to be told to submit to husbands; they were already submitted. But they did need to be told how to work out mutual submission as Christians. They already had ways of working out submission, the submission that was forced upon them by the laws and customs of their country. But that way was destructive and not the Christ way.

Our mistake has been to focus on verse 22 as a command for wives and emphasize a non-existent imperative. This has caused us to miss the true emphasis on the two adverbs, *as* to the Lord and *in everything*, which contain the real advice to wives—the how-to of mutual submission.

Culture

In chapter 5 we looked briefly at Greek marriage. We saw that the first-century Greeks did not usually marry for the reasons we do today. A wife was the means to have a legal heir, and she was a manager for the husband's household. Companionship was not to be expected.

The temptation within a society such as theirs was for those with power to oppress and degrade those under them. Those who were oppressed—wives, children, and slaves— were tempted to retaliate. They also had power of a sort; it was a power to destroy and spoil and waste the resources and harm the reputation of those over them.

Almost everyone, wherever he or she is on the hierarchical ladder, has power. And they use it. For example, in those times the slave could be good when the master was looking, but when the master's back was turned, the slave could go about his work slowly, wastefully, destructively. Today power is still used in destructive ways by those on all levels.

Legally, the Greek wife had few rights. She was personally restricted and could be denied whatever her husband did not want to give her. But she could get back at him. Paul told those wives that if they wanted to live in this new Christ way in unity with other members of Christ's body, they must not use opportunities that came their way for discrediting their husbands. Instead, they must have the same kind of respectful demeanor toward their husbands as they had toward Christ. They would never try to do Christ harm. Those wives should then be as honorable and conscientious toward their husbands as the church was toward Christ.

Savior of the Body

How was the husband the head of his wife in that place and at that time? He was the source of life, the most honorable member of the family, and the family's public representative. He had power over his wife, a power that society gave him because he was male. He was believed to be a superior being; the power and position were automatically his. Greek husbands were used to accepting all the advantages that came with being head of their wives. They were the privileged class. How would mutual submission work itself out in their lives?

As he had appealed to the wives to imitate the attitude and manner of the church in its honor toward Christ, Paul now appealed to the husbands to imitate Christ's treatment of the church. The husband was to see himself as the *savior of the body,* as protector and nourisher, and as one who would raise his wife to a level beside him. Paul said the man was to love his wife as his own body. It doesn't seem so strange to us for a man to love his wife this way, but for them it was not just revolutionary—it was astounding. Greek husbands didn't think of their wives as persons to love. When one of them did talk about his wife as though she were worthy of real love, he was thought to be a bit strange, as witnessed by this quote from Plutarch's *Dialogue on Love.*

> "Oh", said Protogenes, "as this union [marriage] is necessary for the propagation of mankind, legislators must ob-

viously promote it to the people. But not one whit of true love enters the gynaceum. I certainly do not give the name 'love' to the feeling one has for women and girls any more than we would say that flies are in love with milk, bees with honey, or breeders with the calves and fowl which they fatten in the dark. . . . Love inspired by a noble and gifted soul leads to virtue through friendship, but desire felt for a woman leads at best to nothing more than the fleeting enjoyments and pleasures of the body. . . ."

Plutarch's father disagrees with the commonly held opinion:

It is true that sex without love is like hunger or thirst; it is a mere satisfaction of a need and leads nowhere. . . . As I have just demonstrated, the two sexes have the same nature. So, Daphnaeus, in defense of them both, we shall refute Zeuxippus' argument. He identifies love with those immoderate desires which lead the soul to debauchery, not because he believes this himself but because he has heard it said by bitter men who know nothing of love. Some of these ensnare women with the lure of a little money, then deliver them with the money over to the drudgery of housework, sordid account-keeping, and day-long bickering, and generally treat them like servants. Others, more interested in having children than in a wife, do as the male cicada does which lays its seed on an onion or some other vegetable; they get the first female to hand with child, gather the fruit, and say good-bye to the marriage; or else, if they do let it drag on, pay no attention to it, having no interest in loving or being loved.

On the contrary, physical union with the wife is a source of friendship, a sharing together in a great mystery. Sensual delight is brief, but it is like a seed from which day by day there grow between husband and wife consideration for each other, kindness, tenderness, and confidence.[3]

The unity in marriage which the second speaker sees as "a great mystery" parallels the statement of Paul in Ephesians 5:32: "This is a profound mystery," Paul says, "but I am talking about Christ and the church." I do not know what the connection, if any, is between these two statements, one from Plutarch's *Dialogue on Love* and the other from Paul, which seem to be expressing the same thought. Did Paul refer to the origins of this idea about love in marriage that the Greeks were just beginning to talk about, showing Christians that they could partake in this mystery both in their marriages and in a more profound way as believers in union with Christ?

Ephesians 5:25–27

> Husbands, love your wives, just as Christ loved the church and gave himself up for her to make her holy, cleansing her by the washing with water through the word, and to present her to himself as a radiant church, without stain or winkle or any other blemish, but holy and blameless.

The Water Cleansing

These verses have been explained to husbands as requiring some kind of super-human love from them that has as its effect the spiritual purification and growth of their wives, thus making husbands responsible for their wives' spiritual well-being as well as their physical state. But there is a more likely possibility. There is a marriage custom from ancient Greece that sheds some light on this passage.

While doing research for a previous book, I was reading along in a work entitled *Women in Greece and Rome* and came to a section about marriage preparation among Greek women which has a bearing on this passage in Ephesians.

> Before the wedding day the bride-bath took place, in Athens in the spring of Kallirrhoe and in other cities in holy rivers or springs. For this purpose a *lutrophoros* was used, a tall vessel with two handles. If anyone died unmarried, this vessel was set up on the grave in order to grant this holy and important ceremony to the dead.
>
> On the morning of the wedding the bride was ceremoniously washed and clothed, and she donned the bridal wreath and veil.[4]

By means of this pagan Greek ritual the bride was presented to the bridegroom spiritually clean from washing in the sacred spring and physically clean from the washing on the wedding day. She was therefore without spot or blemish, pure and holy. I believe Paul is again contrasting the Christ way and the pagan way, this time by means of a marriage custom familiar to them all—in fact, one they had probably participated in themselves. He is saying that Christ, by means of His Word, makes possible a cleansing that is continuous and complete and far better than that which the pagan worship could provide. Then Paul refers back to the husband to show him that he must not settle for the pagan attitude toward his bride, but must give her the best he has to offer—himself. He is to love her as his own body, just as Christ loves the church enough to give her the best He has—His word and membership in His body.

Rather than teaching that a man was responsible for his wife's spiritual life and growth, Paul was saying that he should give her his best, as Christ gives His best to the church. The Greek husband could do that by elevating his wife up to share with him as an equal (as his own body).

The Analogy Between Christ and the Church and Husband and Wife

Not long ago I sat across the table from a young man at a banquet and we began talking about one of the papers we had heard read that afternoon on ordination for women. From there we moved eventually to a discussion about equality in marriage. I told him I thought the Bible made a good case for equality between husband and wife. He said, "But that ruins the analogy of Christ and the church." I have heard people say something to that effect before. So let's look at this analogy and see what it is all about.

Analogies are useful for one thing only—for *illustrating*. An analogy is a teaching tool, a way to draw a picture to make something more clear to the listeners by showing them something they understand and saying, "It's like that." But it is always only *like* that; it never *is* that because there are no perfect analogies. Unless in all ways the two sides of the analogy are exactly alike, it can only serve as an illustration; it cannot prove anything. In the analogy between Christ and the church and husband and wife the comparisions are not exact.

| Christ = perfect | husband = imperfect |
| church = imperfect | wife = imperfect |

| Christ = unchangeable | husband = changeable |
| church = changeable | wife = changeable |

One set contains a member that is infallible and the other contains none that are. Another interesting difference is that in the case of husband and wife the marriage has already taken place, but in the case of Christ and the church the bride is a promised bride whom the bridegroom will claim at His Second Coming. The marriage of Christ and the church has not yet taken place.

Christians should never base a premise or practice on analogy, but only on principle. Analogies break down since they in themselves are imperfect, but principles are unchanging and able to be interpreted and applied in differing social situations. Further, analogies may be sound only in terms of conditions existing in a certain historical period. Changes in customs make the analogies useless even for the purposes of illustration unless their original use is understood.

The Meaning of Head

I began this chapter by looking for the meaning of *head* in English and asking if our English definition is adequate to define the meaning of *head* in the New Testament. I conclude that it isn't. *Head* meant different things to the people to whom the New Testament was originally written. It meant origin, source, and honor, not leadership and authoritarian rule.

I do not see the New Testament usage of the word *head* awarding husbands authority or leadership positions over their wives as a God-given office men are to occupy in marriage. This seems to be our current idea of what *headship* means, and I see no adequate biblical support for this concept. But there is a relevant tie-in between the meaning of *head* for husbands then and husbands today. The tie-in is power over others and what one does with that power.

In the world of first-century Greece, husbands enjoyed

power, privilege, and advantage over wives because they were believed to be superior to women. A man's position as head (origin, source, honor) awarded him advantage because he was believed to be more important and better quality material than his wife. Paul gave Greek husbands a new way to use this advantage which their society gave them. They were to see it as an advantage to share, to use as a means of service to their wives.

Head Today

The favored position husbands and men in general still have over women can be traced back to the same foundations as those giving Greek men power over women. The belief that men are superior, more important is not dead by any means. Only in comparatively recent times has the church changed its stance on this by saying women are inferior *positionally* instead of *in essence*.

Our society gives men advantages over women too—perhaps not as many as in the day of the New Testament, nor are all of them so obvious, but they are there. In his book *The Kitchen Sink Papers,* Mike McGrady tells of his wife's experiences with this unequal situation and how he helped her even things up by being an honorary member of her firm as he assumed the alternate identities of Mr. Dempsey and Mr. Young.

> Corinne learned, in the early days, that some companies were reluctant to pay their debts to a mere woman. In fact, this is how I became actively involved in the growing firm. On slow days at the office, I would pick up the telephone and read a small speech that I had typed out. . . .
>
> Interestingly enough, the mythical Mr. Dempsey got paid a great deal more rapidly than the real-life Mrs. McGrady. And he enjoyed certain other advantages. For one thing, no one ever called him "sweetie" or "honey" or ever once said to him, "What's a cute thing like you doing in a big business like this?" Also, no one ever tried to proposition him over the phone or to suggest a late supper where they might discuss the matter to better . . . ah . . . advantage.

As recently as this very morning, I was on the phone reading from a second piece of paper.

"Hello, this is Mr. Young, purchasing agent for Corinne McGrady designs. I'd like to speak to your sales department."

It has been our experience that a male voice can get through to a firm's sales department three times as often as a female voice.

Furthermore, we've learned that there are two prices for plastic. The one Corinne has been paying. And the other one, the lower one, the price she was able to get when she called up and introduced herself as "the secretary for Mr. Young, purchasing agent for Corinne McGrady Designs."[5]

According to the principles in the Scripture passages we have been studying, a husband should use the advantages society gives him to help his wife. Maybe not by inventing imaginary members of an imaginary department in his wife's company, but in ways he can conscientiously use to raise her to his level of effectiveness and opportunity. Sometimes that help can come in the form of action, as in the example just mentioned. But the attitude behind the action is the motivating force that works itself out in many ways, as in the case of Jan Erickson-Pearson, a young women studying for the ministry. She says of her husband:

> I doubt that I would have stuck by my plans for ministry if it weren't for my husband Dave. I have received his respect, support and confidence. When others have tried to pretend that I wasn't really in seminary, he was out there telling people I was a good preacher. When male classmates suggested that my good grades were maybe gifts of sympathetic professors, he reminded me that I earned them. When I got discouraged and decided that I just didn't have the stamina to be a pioneer, he would remind me of my strength and my gifts. When I decide that fixing supper is the biggest challenge I can face, he reminds me of past victories.[6]

And sometimes wives are the ones who can reach down and lift husbands up as equals. Women do have a few advantages over men in this society; there are times and places that women even have the upper hand. Use that advantage to serve and help your husband, lifting him up to share the good things with you, not lording it over him.

And for both husbands and wives: The one who finds himself or herself disadvantaged at any time does not use that position to undercut and hurt the one who has the advantage. Do not be spoilers or oppressors. Be a team of equals, sharing together.

---

1. Lee Anna Starr, *The Bible Status of Woman* (Zarephath, New Jersey: Pillar of Fire, 1955), p. 301.

2. For a fuller treatment of this passage see my book *Woman Be Free,* Zondervan, 1977, Chapter 5.

3. O'Faolain and Martines, *Not in God's Image,* pp. 30-32.

4. Zinserling, *Women in Greece and Rome,* p. 27.

5. Mike McGrady, *The Kitchen Sink Papers* (New York: Doubleday, 1975), p. 4.

6. Jan Erickson-Pearson, "But You Can't Be a Pastor," *Daughters of Sarah* (January/February 1979), p. 6.

TOGETHER

9

Heirs Together

The leveling action of Christian love worked out by the Spirit in mutual submission is a way to unity in the body of Christ. And mutual submission in marriage is a way to unity there too. That is, if we take unity to be harmony—not all singing the same note. We need to be able to share equally in all the ways we can, in work, responsibility, pleasure, and opportunity.

The Problem of Work Roles

One area that is a potential problem for modern marriages is that of work. In the next chapter we will look more closely at some practical ways for sharing work and responsibilities, but for now I want to look at some Bible verses that have been used to insist on a sex-linked work restriction that places women at home as housewives and men outside the home as money earners. We need to examine these verses carefully to see if they do restrict married couples to some kind of work role pattern that is God directed, or if they reflect some other principle that we can understand and apply.

Titus 2:3–5

Likewise, teach the older women to be reverent in the way they live, not to be slanderers or addicted to much wine, but to teach what is good. Then they can train the younger women to love their husbands and children, to be self-controlled and pure, to be busy at home, to be kind, and to be subject to their husbands, so that no one will malign the word of God.

The reason for this instruction is given in the last phrase, "so that no one will malign the word of God." It echoes the sentiments expressed so frequently by Paul, and later by Peter, that believers live exemplary lives before their unbelieving neighbors, not so they would think Christians were better than they but so they would not think they were worse. The attributes encouraged in the passage were those accepted by their contemporaries as qualities good women should have; honorable and admired Greek women behaved in this manner. Christian women were to be respectable and honorable so that the Word of God would not suffer by the association.

Rather than laying down a job description for all young women, to apply throughout the rest of history, this passage reveals the common standard for good behavior for a young woman in first-century Greek culture.

For comparison, here are some instructions from a Greek husband named Isomachus. He married his wife when she was fourteen years old and began his instructions toward making her an ideal wife by saying:

It is your duty to remain at home and send out the slaves whose tasks lie outside the house. You must keep an eye on those who work at home, and check what is brought in from outside. You must share out the money to be spent on everything and pay strict attention to what should remain over, making sure you do not spend in one month as much money as is planned for a year. If the wool is brought into the house to you you must take care that they are clothed who need to be, and you must make sure that the dry grain is properly prepared for eating. . . . One, however, of your responsibilities may not be particularly pleasant for you, namely that when anyone in the house is

sick, you must see to it that they are nursed back to health
. . . you can be sure that the older you get and the more
you are a good helpmate for me and an even better protec-
tress for the children of the house, the more you will be
respected and honored in the house.[1]

Epitaphs of Greek women show the same standards:

Neither clothes nor gold did this woman admire in life,
no, she loved only her husband and industry. Now your
husband Antiphitos adorns your grave instead of your
blooming beauty, Dionysia, and your youth.[2]

The word translated "be subject" in Titus 2:5 is the same
word (*hupotasso*) used throughout the New Testament when
addressing wives. It is a self-volitional "putting oneself under
the other." Women were never given a command to submit
unconditionally; rather, the submitting was something each
decided for herself. Husbands were never told to submit their
wives to themselves or demand this submissive behavior. It
was an attitude and behavior wives were instructed to live out
for the sake of their good reputation and also (in the case of
mutual submission) for the sake of unity. This is the same term
used in Ephesians 5:21 to call all believers to mutual submission to each other.

First Timothy 5:14 has also been used to prove that the
only worthy occupation for a Christian married woman is that
of housewife. This belief finds its current expression in books
that guarantee total happiness and fulfillment (and successful
marriages) to women who will be housewives only and spend
their time staying home and doing housework. They see passages like this and the one in Titus as divine mandates for all
women for all time.

1 Timothy 5:14

So I counsel younger widows to marry, to have children,
to manage their homes and to give the enemy no opportunity for slander.

There is that word *slander* again, the concern that wom-
en's behavior should not discredit the faith by disreputable

and dishonorable actions. Earlier in the context of this passage
Paul describes the kind of bad behavior he wants to prevent:
"Besides, they get into the habit of being idle, and going about
from house to house. And not only do they become idlers, but
also gossips and busybodies, saying things they ought not to"
(v. 13).

Even if this were a mandate for all young women for all
time, we are mistaken if we think it involves the kind of life-
style presented in contemporary books which tell wives to let
husbands make all the decisions while they keep a good
house, look pretty, and smell nice. There is an interesting
word in this passage that reveals the kind of job the Greek wife
had. The word *oikodespotein* is the word translated "manage
their homes" here. It has the same root meaning as our word
despot. It shows the very real power and responsibility the
Greek woman had at home. She often managed a large household with many workers. Her life resembled that of the woman
of Proverbs 31 more closely than it does that of the modern
American housewife. This quote from an early Roman source
will illustrate what was expected of a wife then.

> Delia (said I) will guard the reaper's band;
> Delia will keep, when hinds unload the vine,
> The choicest grapes for me, the richest wine;
> My flocks she'll count, and oft will sweet deign
> To clasp some prattler of my menial train:
> With pious care will load each rural shrine,
> For ripened crops a golden sheaf assign,
> Cates for my fold, rich clusters for my vine:
> No, no domestic care shall touch my soul:
> You, Delia, reign despotic o'er the whole![3]

This Roman bridegroom had high hopes for an easy life after
aquiring Delia; he hoped she would take care of everything
from work to worship of the proper gods for ensuring a good
crop.

These Bible passages do not set up some kind of norm for
woman's work. Instead, they reflect what was generally considered to be honorable and praiseworthy for women then.
The lesson or principle for wives now seems to be that they

should live honorable and respectable lives both for the sake of their reputations and the reputation the gospel will have as a result of their being known as Christians. The same, of course, should be true for husbands.

Women not only worked at home, as did Delia, but also worked in the way of Priscilla who made tents with her husband Aquila. These two worked at their trade with the apostle Paul either in their home or possibly in a market stall or shop. They were co-workers in their trade as well as in the work of the gospel. Priscilla's name is often mentioned first, as it is in Acts 18 where it tells how she and Aquila instructed Apollos in the Christian faith. This probably means Priscilla had the greater part in the task as word order in Greek is used for emphasis, with the more important word coming first in the sentence, and women would normally be mentioned after their husbands. Obviously Priscilla and her husband could share both work and ministry, and Priscilla could even come first in teaching ability.

Heirs Together of the Grace of Life

In the same way, you wives, be submissive to your own husbands so that even if any of them are disobedient to the word, they may be won without a word by the behavior of their wives, as they observe your chaste and respectful behavior. And let not your adornment be external only—braiding the hair, and wearing gold jewelry, and putting on dresses; but let it be the hidden person of the heart, with the imperishable quality of a gentle and quiet spirit, which is precious in the sight of God. For in this way in former times the holy women also, who hoped in God, used to adorn themselves, being submissive to their own husbands. Thus Sarah obeyed Abraham, calling him lord, and you have become her children if you do what is right without being frightened by any fear.

You husbands likewise, live with your wives in an understanding way, as with a weaker vessel, since she is a woman; and grant her honor as a fellow-heir of the grace of life, so that your prayers may not be hindered (1 Peter 3:1–7 NASB).

This passage has been used to guarantee wives of unbelieving husbands that they could earn their husbands' salvation by their own complete submission to their husbands demands. I have heard this taught to the extreme of telling a Christian woman that God would not allow her to be subjected to abuse because her husband would be so overwhelmed by his wife's self-sacrifice that he would not ask her to do anything that would be bad for her. Don't you believe it!

The latter part of the passage has been used to threaten husbands to the effect that if they didn't get along with their wives in some mystical way God wouldn't listen to *any* of their prayers. Don't you believe that either.

By seeing these verses, which contain valuable principles, as merely the vehicles for commands we lose their real content. They are tools to help us deal with our problems here and now, but we obscure the message by trying to misapply it. So we not only suffer from imposing a burden unnecessarily, but also from the ommission of the real help offered us.

This passage is found in a context of instruction to Christians who were experiencing such severe persecution that they were losing heart and hope. Peter was trying to encourage them and to give them practical advice for minimizing that persecution. He told them to be honest and upright and to obey the laws. He told them to stop their old dishonest behavior, that there was no law against doing right. In other words, they deserved some of the bad treatment they were getting. He then addressed slaves and told them to do a good job of serving their masters; thus they would spare themselves trouble and be good witnesses too. Peter then turned to wives who, having unbelieving husbands, found themselves in much the same position as slaves with unbelieving masters. His instruction was to help them know how to live their faith before husbands in the way most likely to get good results.

A woman in a situation like that was in a very difficult spot. Her husband could make her life extremely miserable. She, in turn, would be tempted to use any method she could to minimize the trouble or to reach him and get him to listen to "the Word."

Peter cut through to the heart of the problem, telling these women it would not be easy. They must live lives which would reveal the new reality within. They must live out the fruit of the Spirit (a gentle and quiet spirit), rather than trying to impress their husbands with gaudy dress and ornamentation.

And there is a reason why these women would have been inclined to use eye-catching clothing and fancy hairdos to try for their husband's attention. The people addressed by Peter in this letter lived in territory ruled by Rome. The Roman matron of the day was fashion pacesetter for the whole empire, and she rose to the occasion with gusto.

> Roman ladies loved ornamentation. Some of them festooned themselves—this was especally true of the less distinguished women—with fortunes in precious stones and gold ornaments. Pearls, emeralds, beryls and opals were much prized, while jewelry of glass, amber, and coral was preferred by the middle class. Forty million sesterces was the value of the jewelry of Lollia Paulina, one of Caligula's wives.[4]

It required a full-time slave just to construct and maintain their elaborate hairdos and to dress and undress the matron. But the Roman matron was not just preoccupied with clothing, hair, and ornaments; she was interested in gossip also. The picture presented of the ostentatious woman of Rome is one of a shallow, materialistic person who filled her life with trivialities.

For a Christian woman, desperately trying to appeal to her husband, to have adopted the manners and dress of these fashionable women would have been worse than useless. It would have diverted the husband's attention from the central issue of what Christ had done in her life.

Sarah is given as an example of a woman who trusted in God and obeyed her husband, addressing him with a title of respect similar to our word *sir*. She behaved toward her husband in a respectful, conciliatory manner, trusting in God to help her. Sarah "obeyed" Abraham, it says in 1 Peter 3:6. But Abraham also "obeyed" Sarah. The root meaning of the word here translated "obeyed" is the same as the one in Genesis 21:12 translated "hearken" or "listen." The meaning is, from that land of slaves and masters, "I hear, and it is understood that I will do it." There was no way of simply saying "obey." If you "heard," you obeyed. In the case of Abraham and Sarah there was a mutuality or reciprocity of some sort. God told Abraham to "hearken" to Sarah too.

The words to husbands that follow those to wives speak to the same issue—a believing husband with an unbelieving wife. But he had an opposite problem. He wanted to reach the wife whom he may have mistreated and abused for many years. She would not listen to him. His prayers for her conversion went unanswered. What was he to do? Peter told the man to do two things to prevent hindering those prayers for his wife.

First, he was to treat her with respect as the "weaker vessel." Some commentators feel this refers to the then-common idea that woman was "weaker" in every way, substandard material, and the husband should take that into account and not expect too much from her. But there is another possibility that seems more likely. Let me refer to 1 Thessalonians 4:3–5, where the word *vessel* is used in a sexual sense.

> For this is the will of God, your sanctification; that is, that you abstain from sexual immorality; that each of you know how to possess his own vessel in sanctification and honor, not in lustful passion, like the Gentiles who do not know God (NASB).

Now in the passage in Peter the husband was told to be considerate of his wife and treat her with respect as the *weaker vessel*. This might refer to the need for husbands to be considerate of their wives sexually, to realize that women were vulnerable to sexual abuse and misuse in ways men were not. A man might not realize that his past sexual mistreatment of his wife was a major factor in her rejection of him and his faith. And she might not find it easy to tell him this. So, his first concern should be for her comfort and sensibilities and preferences sexually.

Sexual relationships between those husbands and wives were probably none too good in the best of circumstances, so it is easy to visualize the difficulties women might have had in a bad marriage situation. Plutarch encouraged a husband of a good wife to have sexual intercourse three times a month in order to reduce marital tensions. This was supposedly for the wife's benefit since the husband had access to slaves and prostitutes for his sexual needs. This could have been a prime area for needed change in a Christian relationship.

Finally, the husband was told to "grant her honor as a fellow-heir of the grace of life." He was to *grant* her this honor; otherwise she did not have it. And how could she be a fellow-heir? He had to lift her up and treat her as an equal, a co-heir with him in life. He would be treating her in an uncommon way, but he would be living out his faith, a faith which leveled all social barriers, even those between husbands and wives.

So here we have another plea for mutuality. Husbands and wives would be living lives of mutual submission. A husband could reach down to his wife to lift her up, with consideration, to an equal place with him. And the wife would see at last that her husband's faith was real, that it indeed had a new life to offer her. Thus, his prayers would be answered.

But was this a guarantee? I don't think so. It was a guideline. Peter didn't put in an escape clause or a disclaimer because he didn't need to. He knew that if anything would work, this would. It isn't a magic formula, but a biblical principle to live by. It is saying, in effect, "I reach up to you with the best I have to give in conscientious and respectful living." Or, "I reach down to you with the best I have to give in order to mirror my faith and lift you up to share with me all that God gives us." And that's being "heirs together."

In another culture the problems might be different, but the principle would be the same: live your Christianity from within and do not put on an external show of pretense. And don't think you can "talk" Christianity to someone under you; you have to live it and share equality.

In marriages today that might mean opening your hearts to each other—wives being honest with their husbands, and husbands really listening. This could involve sharing feelings about sexual discomfort or any number of other areas of the relationship. It might mean sharing opportunities with each other—mothers sharing child care and husbands sharing educational opportunities or work responsibilities. Years ago when my husband was a student at Talbot Seminary, a woman I knew and admired shared this personal experience with some of us student wives one evening. She said, "When our children were small, I tried to free my husband as much as I could from home duties so he could do his work unhindered. I wouldn't do that again, if I had it to do over. I think I denied him some of the pleasures of caring for his children, getting to know all those things mothers are there to see." She advised us to let our husbands share in child care as much as possible. I think she was right about that. It is not doing a man a favor to do his fathering for him, even though it may seem so at the time.

What can it mean to you to be heirs together? How can you apply the principles in these verses to your own relationship? As you think about ways you can reach out to each other and share the best you enjoy as individuals, remember that sharing means more than cutting the piece of cake in two equal slices. It involves your whole attitude toward the other person. Sharing may involve cultivating the *desire* to share. You cannot force yourself to want to share, but you can think about it and you can pray about it. Remember all the ways you are equal persons in God's estimation; then equalize your life to fit His opinion, not that of society around you.

1. Zinserling, *Women in Greece and Rome*, pp. 28-29.
2. Ibid., p. 29.
3. Ibid., p. 55.
4. Ibid., p. 71.

HEIRS

TOGETHER

10

10

Working It Out

You have to take life as it happens,
But you should try
To make it happen the way you want to take it.
German saying

That's true of marriage. But you can make it happen a lot more the way you want to take it than you may have thought possible. Applying the equalizing principle of mutual submission to your marriage relationship can make the difference.

When people hear references to equalitarian marriage, they are sometimes put off by the idea, thinking it must be an unwieldy way to live. They say things like, "How can you be equal? People aren't equal. If we tried to be equal, it would be ridiculous. My wife would have to mow half the lawn and I would have to cook half the meals!" And they are right, of course. That would be ridiculous—unless that was what they both really wanted. Then it would be fine.

But when I say equal, I don't mean "same as." I mean equal in opportunity, equal in value, equal in personhood. I

135

"My *doing* the *cooking and* your *doing the eating is not* my *idea of sharing chores!*"

Reprinted from *Good Housekeeping* with permission of the artist.

mean a relationship in which neither dominates or misuses the other, where decisions are made together when it is reasonable to do so. I mean a relationship of equal persons not a relationship in which the partners must be carbon copies of each other.

A marriage of equal persons is based on the premise that each person is unique. It flourishes on that fact. It allows both husband and wife to contribute to the union from the richness of all they are. It allows both mates to contribute all their abilities and attributes. And it decrees that *both* decide together, as people with equal say, how their marriage will be and what each will contribute. There is flexibility. They can decide one thing this week and evaluate it next week or tomorrow and decide to do it differently. It is not mainly his *or* her marriage because one is dominant either by temperament and training or by adopted role. It is truly *their* marriage.

I'm sold on equalitarian marriage based on the principle of mutual submission. Not only do I believe it is biblical (which would be reason enough to take it seriously), but I find it affirming of both me and my husband. It is more satisfying in many ways than the traditional hierarchical way. And it is nice to be able to enjoy doing what's right.

There also are practical advantages to an equal relationship in marriage. The problems of the role-playing marriage drop away as both partners are able to grow and develop as persons without wondering if they are getting out of their "role." They are free to share their thoughts and feelings, dreams and problems with each other knowing it is all right to be what they are. This leads to a personal intimacy far beyond that which is possible in a marriage where both are trying to be someone they are not. *For how can I love the real you when you are trying so hard to be someone else. And how can you love the real me when I am trying to be someone else.* These are two lonely people playing games with each other, but never really touching souls. That game can be dropped and left behind. Oh, I don't mean all pretenses and fears will automatically and immediately fall away. But in an increasingly free and accepting atmosphere, more and more they can reveal who they really are until they are confident enough to be themselves completely.

A marriage of equals is something people can grow into rather than force themselves to assume. Getting used to being married is hard enough anyway—learning to live with another person so closely, finding out all those terrible things they didn't know about, like the messes they make and the little inconsiderations that nibble away at the cookie of their "perfect" marriage. If they have to adopt some kind of roles at the same time, marriage can be an uprooting and traumatic experience. Thus, many have felt that their own personalities and beings were eroded away by marriage until they hardly had any of their own self left. This should not be and need not be. In a marriage of equals each person is helped to find, nourish, and develop all he or she is rather than suppress and deny it.

How To Put Equal Marriage Into Practice

Where do we begin? At first glance there seem to be all manner of problems to working out marriage between equals. Who will do the work? Who will make decisions? What if we can't agree? What if we *really* can't agree? Won't the children be confused?

For those who have never thought of marriage in this way before, it seems difficult. In practice it works itself out quite smoothly.

First of all there's the matter of dividing work and responsibilities. These can be divided up between the two of you on a temporary basis. I say temporary because you should get used to the idea that you will want to modify your arrangements as you see better and more satisfying ways to do things.

Dividing Work and Responsibilities

Set aside an hour some evening when you are both in a relatively relaxed and happy state. Then discuss divisions of work and responsibility. You can do it all verbally and remember it, or you might want to make notes to remind yourselves what you decided to try.

First, list the broad areas of responsibility and work that you have in your home: car maintenance, cooking, shopping, yard work, child care, cleaning, bill paying, etc. Then ask yourself: Who has the most competence and/or interest in each of these areas? Does this person want the job, or does he or she want to share it? One of you may be willing to take responsibility for seeing the job is done right but want help in doing the actual work. And if one has skill in an area and would like to train the other so a more equal workload is possible, that can be done too.

Try to divide the work and responsibilities so that each one of you has an equal share, an equal amount of job satisfaction, and an equal amount of jobs that neither wants to do but are necessary for the running of the household. Or you might agree to hire a third party to do the unwanted jobs. The important thing is to, as honestly as possible, evaluate the work and responsibility and share it fairly.

You may not be 100 percent happy with the results the first time you attempt this, but at least settle on something on a trial basis. Agree on a time to reevaluate the division in the near future, say a week or two or a month from now. When you come back to the subject for your reevaluation, discuss the problems and possible revisions you can make in the plan to improve it.

Decision-making

Dividing up work and responsibility according to competence and interest ensures that the person best fitted to do the job has the power to make sure it is done right. It also avoids all the little disagreements that would arise from having to agree on every small detail because: *Minor decisions are made by the person whose area of work or responsibility the decision falls in.* If the husband has responsibility for car care, he does not need to consult his wife about the kind of wax or gas he buys or when it is to be washed. She can make suggestions and raise objections during an evaluation session, or at any other time for that matter, but minor choices are his to decide. The same would hold true for any other area. This frees both partners from a lot of needless disagreements.

Major decisions are reached together. You must genuinely be able to agree on major decisions. But what if you can't agree? Then you do nothing until you can agree. But what if you *really can't* agree? You wait until you can either compromise, go another direction, or find a satisfactory solution for both of you. That is if the matter under consideration is neither an emergency nor a decision that affects one of you clearly more than the other and would pose hardship for that one if put off indefinitely.

In the case of an emergency, a natural leader arises who will automatically decide if allowed to lead as he or she is capable of doing. For example, in most families when one of the children falls and splits his chin on the sidewalk, one parent automatically grabs a wet washcloth and stops the bleeding while soothing the child and the other parent either stands and stares, goes to pieces, or feels like it. The problem solves itself unless the more capable partner is prevented from acting because they, or the other partner, think it is not their "role" or place to do the acting or deciding. Emergencies are not usually a problem in decision making unless the natural capabilities of the partners are ignored.

If the problem needing a major decision clearly puts one partner in a position of greater need, that partner ought to have the greater say if there is difficulty making the decision.

Most disagreements profit by the "wait until we can agree" method. Suppose the bathroom needs to be painted. It is something both want done, but she wants to paint it blue, which he hates, and he wants to paint it green, which revolts her. If he gives in and agrees to blue (just to be agreeable), every time he walks in that bathroom he will be reminded of how he didn't like that color and will resent her because of it. If she gives in (because he is the decision maker), she will resent him every time she has to enter that revolting green room. But if they leave the room alone until they both want it painted so much that yellow looks good to both of them, then when they see those walls they will be reminded of their ability to agree and get along with each other. Instead of a source of irritation, that bathroom will be a monument to their ability to work together.

But you'll have to be fair about it. No pushing each other around, arguing each other down, high-pressure tactics, or wheedling. It might not be easy to give up all your old ways of getting what you want, so keep your eyes open for them; they will probably crop up. When you see yourself operating in these old ways, admit it, and then try again to decide *without* applying manipulation or force to the other partner.

You might want to read about the kinds of destructive games people play in relationships and how to stop them. *Born to Win* by Muriel James and Dorothy Jongeward is helpful, as is the book *The Mirages of Marriage* by William J. Lederer and

Don D. Jackson. *No-Fault Marriage* by Marcia Lasswell and Norman M. Lobsenz explains ways people operate within their marriages and gives suggestions for making changes. How do you decide whether a decision is a major or a minor one? My husband and I find that if one of us thinks it is major, then it is, whether the other one does or not. Because if one treats it as minor when the other feels it is really important, it will be a source of contention between us. Another way to decide what is major and minor is to set some kind of guideline for yourselves. For example, you could decide that expenditures under a certain amount would not need to be consulted about. The limit is set by the two of you in agreement and changed later if needed. Or you could set up areas you feel are major and assume all other are minor unless something arises to make you change your mind. The important thing here is to be honest with yourself and each other. The object is to make decision making easier and more satisfying, not to see what you can get out of it personally. Remember, this is a team effort, not competition between the two of you.

Setting Goals

You will probably see areas in your marriage that you want to change to make the relationship more equal and satisfying to one or both of you. Let me suggest that you set specific goals to make concrete changes.

Beware of setting up too many goals at once. It is usually easier and more comfortable to grow gradually into a new way of living. Pick out one area that you would like to change, and set a goal that is specific. Set a time limit you want to aim for if the goal lends itself to that, and at the end of this time evaluate your progress toward the goal. Have you been successful? Why? Why not? Do you want to continue toward the same goal if you were not successful, or would you like to focus on another area for now?

It is important to remember that you are working on these changes together so that you evaluate your progress, or lack of it, in an objective manner. If one of you decides the goal is not what they want after all, stop right there and evaluate it. Talk about it until you can agree on some goal, if not this one.

For example, you want to work to equalize the child care load. So you set a goal: for a week father will give the two and four-year-olds their baths, read them a story before bed, and tuck them in. If midway through the week this becomes difficult or impossible because father must be away or the children get sick and want back their familiar routine, drop the goal and choose a new one or put this one off to another time. In other words, improvise as you need to, keeping in mind the larger goal of equalizing both the work and pleasure of child care.

There is a formula for setting and achieving goals that you may find helpful:

1. Set an achievable goal that can be specifically stated.
2. Set a time limit.
3. Determine the first step toward that goal.
4. Take that step.
5. Evaluate. Did you succeed in your efforts? If so, determine the next step and take it. If not, can you think of another way to reach that first step? Do you still want the same goal? If not, proceed to a new goal and take the first step toward it.
6. Evaluate both method and goal after each step, but take only one step at a time.

This method, which I learned from a book called *Choose Success* several years ago, is a workable way to do almost anything. It's secret is flexibility and taking only one step at a time. It will work in making changes in your marriage too.

Relationship Evaluation

There is another kind of evaluating you should do if you want to maintain your marriage of equals in a way that will be satisfying and not deteriorate into old familiar patterns. You should make a continuing practice of getting together to evaluate your marriage.

These can be pleasant, reaffirming times if you remember the following guidelines. Do not evaluate when you are angry about something or in a bad state from some other source. Plan these times specifically. If you don't, the only time you will talk about your marriage will tend to be when there is a problem or when one of you is unhappy about something. There is nothing wrong with having a gripe session or working on a problem (you should do that if you need to), but I am talking about a different type of evaluation.

You need to take stock of your relationship as a whole periodically to see if there are areas you would like to improve, little things you would like to change, or big things you would like to do and need to talk about. You could set up these times on a monthly basis or however often you feel they are desirable. You could make this time an evening out together, or even a weekend away during which you combine pleasure and time together to look at your marriage for ways you can improve it.

Evaluate the changes you have made already and decide what you would like to do next. Get to know each other personally. What do you want for yourselves as individuals? How does that affect or influence your relationship? How can you help each other toward personal goals? What are your strengths? How can your alliance together be made stronger? How can the team be made happier, more secure, and a greater source of pleasure for both of you?

This kind of non-problem-centered dreaming and sharing together can be a nourishing and healing experience. It happens too rarely or not at all in most marriages.

Solving Problems

This sounds like a big order—how to solve problems. I think it will help if I share some methods of solving problems that my husband and I have used successfully. They may be useful for you to try or may serve as idea generators to help you think of more ways yourself. If you want to work problems out together, you can usually find a way.

Define the problem. Often we sense a problem in a general

way or think we know what it is when it is really something
else that is bothering us. I don't mean you should go into all
your past disappointments with each other to try to determine
what it was you didn't like then. Stick to the present. What *is*
the problem now?

Who does the problem belong to? Sometimes just knowing
who owns the problem will tell you who should decide how it
should be solved—or whose responsibility the solution is.

*What are the possible solutions that immediately come to
mind?* Personally, I like writing such things down because it
helps clarify my thinking; also, I don't forget some when there
are several. Write down even those that sound unrealistic because they may be usable after all, or modified, or they may
spark another idea that will work.

Evaluate the possible solutions pro and con. What are the
advantages and disadvantages of each? Are some impossible,
or prohibitive for some reason? Do you want to eliminate
them? Can you think of any others? If not, rate the ones remaining as to desirability from first choice to last.

You may have a workable solution by now, or a tentative
one you can try and then modify later if you need to. You may
not have anything you can use. If not, give yourself some time
to think it over and let it incubate in your mind. Come back to
the process later and begin over. You may have a different
view of the original problem. Or another solution may come to
mind. Or you may see how one of the ones you rejected will
work after all.

At any rate, allowing time for the problem to sit after
preliminary problem solving is often a good idea. Some problems solve themselves given time, others clarify themselves. But
the main reason for waiting is the likelihood that you will be
able to evaluate your possible solutions better after a time lapse.

Some other questions you can ask in problem solving are:
What do each one of the parties involved want? What are their
actual needs? What do they fear? Can you think of ways both
of your needs can be met? Can you avoid the result feared? Can
you agree on a tentative first step?

Quid Pro Quo

This pleasant technique came from the book *The Mirages of Marriage,* and we have been using it in our family for several years. It is not unusual for one of the children to say to each other or to us, "How about a *quid pro quo?*" The words are Latin for "this for that." It is a way of getting something you want in an open, non-manipulative way from someone who may not necessarily want to give it to you but might take something from you in exchange. It must be used sparingly as an auxiliary way of solving minor problems, not as a way of dealing with everything. If you used *quid pro quos* for everything, you would have a legalistic and stiff relationship. But it is fun for occasional use.

It goes like this: Mary really hates to go into the bathroom to brush her teeth and see the tube of toothpaste squished up all over. It is a small thing, but it bothers her. So she asks Jim if he would please not do it. Jim says it doesn't matter much to him, and if he remembers he squeezes it from the bottom. But he usually doesn't remember. So Mary goes back to Jim and says, "Jim, I would like a *quid pro quo.* I would like to trade your squeezing the toothpaste neatly from the bottom for me not using your razor any more to shave my legs." She hasn't thought the razor thing very important either, but knew he didn't like it. They agree, both try harder, and that's that. But if Jim doesn't care that much about the razor, he may suggest another option for Mary. He may ask that she not hang her nylons to dry over the bathtub—or something else. The important point is that they must finally agree on a trade that is of equal value to both of them. Sometimes you can't find anything to trade, so you just drop it and use it another time when you can both find suitable things to trade.

Sometimes someone wants a special treat or favor but doesn't want to ask the other to do it for nothing. In that case it might be a plate of fudge traded for a trip to the grocery store. A *quid pro quo* is mutually rewarding.

Fighting Constructively

I'm going to be realistic and assume all marriages involve disagreements, fights, and arguments. What we need to know is how to fight constructively.

Most of us don't know how to fight right. We fight dirty. And when we are done fighting, we don't know how to stop gracefully.

Here are some guidelines for contructive results: Limit the fight to what is immediately at stake. Stick to the issue. If someone brings up a side issue, insist it be tabled for another time. Say what you really feel, but don't be brutal. Use what are called "I messages." Say, "I hate getting places late; it embarrasses me." Not, "You are always making me late."

Solve the problem; don't try to vanquish an opponent. If you have several grievances, save them until this matter is settled. Agree to write them down individually and share them when you aren't angry. Then work to solve them and find ways of improving any problem areas you uncover.

Cool off if you need to. Sometimes you will profit from a good brisk walk or jog, or cleaning out a closet or two. It helps to discuss a disagreement rationally when you aren't so full of anger. You can work off a lot of hostility and anger just by using your large muscles in some harmless activity. It might even be a good way to get that job done you've been putting off.

We'll assume you have cooled down, stated the problem as you see it, gotten the other person's viewpoint, aired your feelings, and refrained from dragging in side issues. Now can you look for a common ground on which you can stand together? Can you move toward mending the torn place between you? Is there a first step either of you can take? A step both can take together?

What about forgiveness? Make sure it is constructive too. I would like to share something I learned from David Augsburger in a lecture years ago. He said (paraphrased by me and my memory) that we can coerce and dominate each other in the matter of forgiveness as much as in the act that prompted the need for forgiveness. If we insist that the other person forgive us, since we "apologized," that can be coercion. Or we can condescendingly say, "I forgive you," and that is oppressive. Augsburger said forgiveness does not reside in the words themselves. Rather, the best kind of forgiveness consists of that move toward the other that says (whether by word or deed), "I realize the broken relationship exists between us, and I am willing from this moment to move toward mending it and making right what is wrong as well as I am able." The other then reaches back to the partner and says, in effect, "I also will do my part to mend the broken relationship."

I like that. Forgiveness is not something we can demand of others or hand out like a royal gift. It is a willingness to mend the break and take responsibility for righting whatever wrong has been done.

So forgive each other as you are able, in a good way. That is the best way to fight. And to stop. It keeps you equal persons, and it is not destructive. In fact, its end result is often constructive.

What else is nice about working it out? There are fringe benefits to equal marriage, good things that happen as a result of living as equals.

HEIRS TOGETHER

TOGETHER

11

11

Fringe Benefits

When I was thinking of the ways equal marriage has changed our family and other families I know who live like this, I realized there are a lot of extras I have been enjoying but didn't connect with the equality bit. I want to tell you about them now to encourage you and give you something else to look forward to if you decide to live more equally.

Family Benefits

A marriage of equal people affects the whole family because you eventually realize you must treat your children as equal people too. This does not mean that you express that equality in exactly the same way as you would with another adult. You do not give them responsibilities they are not capable of handling. But it does make a difference—several differences.

First of all, children learn by watching you handle division of labor, disagreements, problem solving, mutual respect. You may find them asking for more participation in the decision-making process.

We found that as parents we became less willing to make all our children's decisions for them as we got more into a relationship of equals with each other. I found myself balking at having to hand down and enforce decisions about chores, homework, and privileges.

Now the children in our family did not always want to have a *responsible* part in the decision-making process. They were a bit lazy about it at first. They would have liked it better if we parents had decided; then if they didn't like the decision they could fuss about it or argue until they got what they wanted in the first place, or at least softened the blow.

We discovered that our children were playing a game, in which we unwittingly participated, called "Make Me Do It Mom/Dad." The object was to see how many ways they could drag out a job or a bedtime or avoid a responsibility. If we insisted, they made excuses, complained that we were unfair, or used any other ploy they thought might work. It was a kind of, "Well, folks, we are your responsibility; you just have to make us do what we should." The way we solved this was a spin-off from our own equalization as marriage partners. We instituted a family council. We tried it out two or three times unsuccessfully before we hit on a way that worked for our family (probably also until we finally decided that we would *make* it work).

Now we all get together once a week for a few minutes and air complaints, assign work, and set goals. We, as parents, told the children that we did not intend to consider all the work as basically ours, that we are a family and we believe the work should be fairly divided and done with quality results. At first there were quite a few disruptive jokes, but eventually they became convinced we really intended to share both the work and the decision making with them.

We don't make changes unless we can all agree. Each has equal access to the decision making and discussion, and we try to avoid politicking and stick to the issue at hand. And it is working. I'll give you an example. We all share household work. The children rotate dishwashing and bathroom, cleaning among them. Nobody is too keen on cleaning the bathroom, but now the attitude toward the work has changed. It is no longer, "If it gets bad enough, mom will make me do it. Or she might even do it herself if she is embarrassed about it being so dirty." Now there is a cry of, "Who has the bathroom this week?" And it isn't mom doing the objecting because they know they are all getting cheated if it is dirty. They have finally realized it is *their* bathroom too. And if it isn't clean, they have to live in the mess. And they have to clean it next week with double the work.

I'm not saying everyone should have a family council or that it is a cure-all. It is just one way equalization in our marriage has affected our family. And it has been a good influence.

I think you will find yourself being more considerate of your children as individuals under a more equal regime. It is hard on your conscience to be the heavy-handed father or mother when you are experiencing the liberating effects of a more equal relationship with your husband or wife. You want to help the child be himself or herself rather than impose your own ideas. Don't misunderstand me though; I don't mean you just turn them loose and let them grow up like weeds. Children need parents to guide them and set boundaries they are not knowledgeable or experienced enough to set for themselves. But much of what passes as parental concern is really just domination of someone smaller than you are. Once in awhile almost every parent catches himself or herself doing it. You tend to catch yourself more, and be more uncomfortable with domination, when you are not living in a dominant-submissive relationship with your spouse.

I now find myself encouraging my children to solve their own problems. I don't know if equalizing marriage has anything to do with it or not, but I suspect it does. In an equal relationship one has more hope that problems can be rationally solved, that it is possible to do something about a bad or uncomfortable situation. It not only encourages cooperation, but also self-reliance.

Somehow, seeing my children as whole and equal persons instead of little people I must control and mold as an authoritarian parent gives me a more realistic view of their capabilities and limitations. I can empathize with their problems without having to take over and solve them. Perhaps, too, equalitarian marriage frees me to spend more emotional energy on a positive relationship with others. I am not so stressed with unresolved conflicts with my mate that I haven't enough of myself left to share with my children and to see when a problem *does* need my parental help and control.

I asked our children if they have noticed a difference in our family as a result of the kind of marriage Stan and I have. And did they like the difference?

Three agreed that they liked the differences they could see; one was rather noncommittal.

Jon, who is eleven, said, "You can ask either parent if you want something. You don't have to wait for the one who makes the final decisions to come home and decide."

Ann, nineteen, said, "You don't have everyone conspiring together to convince dad to let you have or do what you want. There is not so much secrecy as in families where they are always saying, 'Don't tell dad, but. . . .' I don't think the mother gets the same respect as the father in a family where her decisions aren't as important. She isn't allowed to make the important ones."

Dave, sixteen said, "Everyone seems more equal. There is no dictator ruling over the family. You are more likely to get what you want because both parents contribute a wider understanding and interest than if only one made the final decision. So you have more chance of someone being able to identify with why you want it and how you feel."

The above interviews were done while Dan, eighteen, was away on a trip. In my eagerness to incorporate his comments I made the mistake of asking him his opinion soon after he got home from a ten-hour drive and two almost sleepless nights. "Doesn't make any difference to me," he said and stalked off to bed.

Well, three out of four isn't bad. I think I can say they recommend it. Mostly.

Another value for the children is that skills in dividing responsibility, problem solving, and empathizing at home prepare them for living more harmoniously with others when they leave home for college or are on their own. It helps them learn the democratic process.

In *The Kitchen Sink Papers* Mike McGrady tells how his family equalized work and responsibility during the year he spent as the housewife of the family. At the end of the year they drew up a family contract spelling out their new divisions of labor and responsibilities.

He says, "What we are after is an equal distribution of rights and responsibilities, a classless family." He goes on to say that their division of work and responsibility is right for their own family but that other families would need to work things out to suit their own needs. But I think we could all agree with the *General Philosophy* which bound it all together and appears right above the signatures of all the members of the family.

1. Never do anything that bothers, hurts or interferes with another member of the family.
2. It's a home, not a house, and it should be treated accordingly.
3. Do unto others as you would have them do unto you.[1]

That sounds like mutual submission, doesn't it?

Communication

Everybody is always talking about the need for communication, but nobody seems to define what it is. Certainly it is not just talking with someone or being with them without watching television or reading a book. It is sending and receiving true messages in a pleasant and meaningful way. Communication is being open and vulnerable. And it is better between equals. In fact, maybe the *only* way communication is possible is between equals. How can you communicate without honesty? And how can you be honest unless you refuse to

distort your own self? And how can the other person really
hear you unless they are being their own self without roles
superimposed?

Do I mean by this that equalitarian marriage makes communication simple and always possible without problems?
No. Not for my husband and me anyway. But it is easier to
break through the barriers that prevent real communication
when we can drop games and manipulations and state our real
feelings and needs. We fight and disagree intensely sometimes. But we have a basis for meeting to discuss our differences and work out a way to still be friends and partners.

I know so many families whose members cannot be open
with each other. Their communication is a tangled maze worthy of any soap opera. I'm not much of a soap opera buff
myself, but I have watched one of them enough times to know
the general drift of the various plots and who is married to
whom and who was to whom before who is now was. And I
came to the conclusion that this program has one main
theme—*well-meaning deception.* Everybody on "All My Children" seems to get into trouble because they have covered up
the truth, stretched it a bit, or downright lied—and usually
"for their own good."

That same deception is so common in Christian families
that it could be the number one reason for communication
breakdowns.

I knew one family in which this was an intriguing
sidelight to knowing them. Everyone was communicating on
two levels. There was the actual conversation, which was
pleasant and jovial, but underneath there was another river
flowing. They spent a lot of time figuring out "what he/she
really meant." It took me awhile to realize this was going on,
that fights, jealousies, and conflicts were all being waged subtly underneath their peaceful exterior.

I came from a family where people got mad and blew up,
told each other what they thought, let it blow over, and went
on without too much internalized residue. But in this family
there was a constant back water of unresolved conflicts and

anger because they could not meet openly as real people and discuss their problems. They had to pretend to be someone else, to keep to their prescribed roles and "place." They were afraid to communicate honestly with each other so they missed the closeness they could have had.

You can't live like that and be equal persons. And you can't really communicate when you live as they did.

Intimacy

This is another fringe benefit that is hard to define. You know when you have it. It's that feeling you get when you snuggle up with a three-year-old and read him a story and he looks up into your eyes and says, "Daddy, you know what . . .?" It's the feeling a mother gets breast-feeding her baby in a relaxed and cozy place with just the two of them there caring about each other. It's what we all long for—a communication that is heart to heart, skin to skin.

An equal marriage will not automatically produce intimacy, but I don't think you can have true intimacy without a marriage of equal persons. If one of you has control, the weak partner will be forced to use games to get what he or she needs from the other. They may play games like "If You Really Loved Me You Would." The weak partner cannot feel free to state needs and wants and expect that they will be discussed or considered as equal to the needs and wants of the dominant partner. Any time we must use ploys to get what we need, we destroy the possibility for intimacy. Intimacy involves being totally open and vulnerable to the other person at that moment. We must feel safe enough in the other's presence to risk that vulnerability.

> I am so happy with you
> I can discuss all my thoughts, or
> I don't have to say anything
> You always understand.
>
> I am so relaxed with you
> I don't need to pretend
> I don't need to look good
> You accept me for what I am.

I am so strong with you
I depend on you for love
But I live my own life
You give me extra confidence to succeed.[2]

Sex

How can you have a whole book on marriage and never discuss the subject of sex? Well, folks, this is it. And it's true —there is a sexual fringe benefit to equalitarian marriage.

We've been talking about being free to be your own self and discover who that self is in a marriage which allows you to be all you are and can be. Sex is a prime area for concealment of true feelings and desires. We are so conditioned by our up-bringing and society's (including the church) messages about sex that by the time we reach marriage our sexuality has been thoroughly repressed or distorted. Some of us have never told *anyone* how we really feel about sex or what we would like sexually. Often we do not even know ourselves what we really think about it. The Christian community is moving toward accepting sexuality as the good gift from God that it is, but we have far to go before all Christians are comfortable with sexual expression, even within marriage.

An equal marriage has several advantages over a hier-archical one when it comes to sex. It may be fun for awhile to pretend that the husband is a Macho Man and the wife is a Fascinating Female, but since people don't fit such stereotypes very well, the day inevitably comes when it becomes a pose. You aren't being real; you long to be yourself and drop the pretenses. In an equal relationship both men and women are free to discover their sexuality as it really is. It is possible to gradually peel away the layers of conditioning and find out what you do like and do not like, to learn to ask for what you want and be free to refuse kindly what you do not.

In marriages of equal people you no longer need to know what some expert thinks women want sexually; you can ask your own wife and have some confidence that she will tell you. You can throw out other people's ideas. If you read that women don't mind if they do not experience orgasm, but you do mind, then you have enough confidence in your own self and partner to believe your own body, not discount it to adapt to someone else's concept of your sexual role.

Rather than focusing on supposed differences between the sexes and what this means sexually, the equal couple is free to focus on each other. They want mutuality in their sexual experiences, not conformity. One can be free to learn what the partner is like and forget preconceived notions. Consideration for the other can replace wondering how you are doing as a sex partner.

Sex can be what you want it to be. What if you had never heard of sex before? What if you had just discovered it? How would you learn about this new thing, live with it, enjoy it?

If you are experiencing problems in your sexual relationship, you can be freer to talk openly about them with each other in the atmosphere of an equal relationship. You can look at it as a problem you share and use problem solving techniques. It is no longer a silent "something is wrong"—or worse, the belief that one of you is inadequate.

The sharing nature of a marriage based on mutual submission brings a consideration and comfortableness to sex that can make it what you want it to be at any given time—fun, physical desire, or a way to express intimacy.

Personal Identity

When I talk to people with equalitarian marriage relationships or read what they have written, I find a recurring comment inserting itself. Living with another person who treats you as a whole, equal person has a liberating effect on what you are able to be as an individual, apart from the relationship.

Women tell me that their husbands have encouraged them to try things they were hesitant to undertake because it seemed beyond their abilities or was unacceptable to others because women "don't do those things." Husbands encouraged their wives to do these things because they knew their wives were capable people; they could see the potential. Again and again, that encouragement and emotional support while undertaking the difficult task has been the key ingredient to making it a positive experience. Sometimes it was the key to making it possible at all.

Men, in turn, confide that they are free to do things they had not attempted before. Their wives have helped them uncover ambitions and feelings they had hidden because they were either unacceptable to their own families when they were growing up or to society at large. Men often find the personal affirmation in an equalitarian relationship liberating for their emotions. It hasn't been acceptable in our culture for men to experience the full range of human emotions. As a result, they have had to push unacceptable emotions down inside and sometimes even convince themselves that those feelings did not exist.

A marriage of equal persons helps us get in touch with who we really are. We dare to believe that our dreams can really come true. We can come out of hiding and be the real us.

In an earlier chapter I talked about the need for personal awareness and growth as a particularly comtemporary need. Equalitarian relationships provide both the personal freedom necessary to allow the individuals room to grow to full potential within the marriage and the support to encourage that growth in spite of setback and opposition from without. We need to be accepted not only for who we are, but for who we can become.

> Any force that stands in the way of our becoming is alien to us. To have someone who shares your closest thoughts and feelings stand in your way is to be tripped on your own doorstep before you have had a chance to try your fortunes in the world. The worst thing one partner can say to the other is, "You kept me from being me."[3]

The mutual acceptance in an equalitarian marriage can even help us become more mature adults. E. Mansell Pattison, a Christian psychologist, in talking about the transition from an immature, childlike image of self to that of an adult says, "Up to this time we talked about external things that define who I am. The move into adult mature identity requires that one be able to surely fix the sense of self as primarily an internal attribute of self. No longer does what I do define who I am. Rather, because of who I am, I now define what I do."[4] He points out that failure to make this transition results in identity crisis when a person must change what he does. Because his identity is still rooted to *what* he does, he doesn't know *who* he is.

If we expect marriage partners to fulfill certain roles and fit into stereotypes, we encourage the immature view of self that can cause problems with personal identity. But to accept the marriage partner as a person who does not need to fit into roles, who does not get his or her identity from what he or she does, is to free the partner to mature and attain a strong sense of personal identity from within that will help them withstand changes. It also promotes a feeling of personal worth and self-confidence which are assets to anyone.

That Something Extra

A certain vitality and comfortableness shine from several equalitarian marriages I have observed. A couple of things I read recently reminded me of the way they are.

If two people living together do not generate a world that is greater than the sum of each of them alone, their union is superficial and static.[5]

Anthropologist Ruth Benedict often wrote about the "co-operative energy" that flows like an electric current through a harmonious group. Similarly, two people working together can achieve more than either could individually using the same amount of time and effort. This effect is called "synergy"—the enrichment, the added strength, the extra hidden ingredient that occurs when a couple complement each other by bridging their differences.

Indeed, the differences are almost as important as the similarities so far as the synergic reaction is concerned. A traveler in a foreign country who fears or fights the differences in its culture does not enjoy his trip nearly so much as the traveler who accepts, respects, and even enjoys those differences. Much the same is true in marriage. If two people are exactly alike (which, of course, no two people are but which some couples seem determined to become), they limit the potential that synergy provides. For differences add not only interest but also strength when both husband and wife have learned how to deal with them.[6]

When I remember being with couples who have a relationship based on mutual submission, seeing each other as individuals who are different from each other and being glad about it, I remember a warmth between them and an electricity unlike the sparks some couples generate because of their volatile connection. There seems to be more *life* in the equal couples. Maybe that's because their arrangement frees the resources of both to contribute to this synergy.

I know I have experienced this feeling of combined strength in my own marriage. I don't always feel it because we don't always live in all the light we have. But I remember thinking just a day or two ago, *I feel so good about everything. It's as though there is a happiness here that is something extra.* It was because we were both doing what we most wanted to do and supporting each other in it, not "just to be kind" but because we had each totally accepted what the other was doing as fine, okay, because that was what that one wanted and needed to do.

Equal marriage isn't a panacea; I don't want you to think that. It won't cure all your marital ills. And you probably won't find it totally without problems in itself. We were all raised with the traditional hierarchical propaganda (and I don't mean that word propaganda in a negative way). Under pressure we tend to revert to the ways we grew up with.

If you find yourself fighting tooth and nail in all the old dirty ways you used to hate to see your parents use, and you think your equal relationship has gone down the drain, don't despair. Just pick yourselves up and start where you are to improve it.

Build a marriage together that is uniquely yours and that you can change to suit your changing needs. Make your marriage what the two of you want it to be and it will be ever-fresh and a source of contentment and joy to you.

Please sift all advice through your own competent minds with the aid of the Holy Spirit. Don't take my advice or that of any other person if it isn't right for you.

In the meantime, you may still have some questions. I hope they are answered in the next chapter.

---

1. McGrady, *Kitchen Sink Papers*, p. 185.

2. Schutz, *I Want to Laugh*, p. 17.

3. David Viscott, *How to Live with Another Person* (New York: Pocket Books, 1974), p. 33.

4. E. Mansell Pattison, "A Psychologist's Perspective on Woman's Role and Status," (tape) Denver Seminary Conference on Women, 1974.

5. Viscott, *How to Live*, p. 32.

6. Marcia Lasswell and Norman M. Lobsenz, *No-Fault Marriage* (New York: Doubleday, 1976), p. 107.

HEIRS
HEIRS
HEIRS
HEIRS
HEIRS

TOGETHER

12

12

Questions
and
Answers

Occasionally I am asked to speak on the subject of biblical equality for women because of my book *Woman Be Free*. When I do, I always try to leave time for discussion because the subject is unusual and there are many questions in people's minds about it.

I enjoy such question and answer times; it is then I find out what people really want to know about the subject. And it is also satisfying to have the answers (when I do).

When I speak on the subject of women and equality in the church, the discussion usually gets around to the subject of equality in marriage because someone almost always says, "If women can be equal in the church, how does this affect marriage?" So I have become accustomed to answering questions on this subject too. Many of the questions that follow were asked in such gatherings. I will begin with one most frequently asked and let the best person for the job answer it.

Questions and Answers

What does your husband think of all this? How does he feel about equal marriage?
Stan says:

I would not have been attracted to Pat in the first place had I not seen in her one who was my equal. The fact that she was pretty was important. But that would have counted for little had she not been bright, decisive, strong in will and character, steady, interesting, full of life and love of adventure, wise, loving, and intelligent. (Now she's embarrassed that she a-greed to let me answer this question!) I saw her and naturally related to her as one who was my equal. What she thought, said, dreamed, wanted, and planned were as important to me as my own ideas. It was her unique individuality that attracted me.

But within a few days of marriage that began to change. Traditional ideas of male leadership and female submissiveness began to take over. It was so ingrained in us that at the time I don't think we really understood what was happening. But two people who had met as equals, initially related as equals, and fallen in love as equals were not living and relating in marriage as equals in *mutual* submission to each other. Is it any wonder we were not happy?

After all too long a time, some years back we began to try to rediscover that original relationship.

How do I like a marriage of equals, living in mutual submission? Well, it really does have all the fringe benefits Pat mentions in the preceding chapter. I also believe it to be biblical, the way God intended marriage to be—and that's important to me. But there is one other thing. Living as equals has given me back the woman I was originally attracted to. It has brought *us* back to the basis for the relationship that *we* originally had. And that is what we both wanted out of marriage, a continuation of our good relationship.

I think my wife and I have a more or less equal marriage relationship without even realizing it. We seem to have evolved it over the years. We make most decisions together and have even divided up the work somewhat as you describe but in a more gradual and not purposeful way. What is wrong with our doing it this way?

Not a thing. More couples probably have equalitarian marriages than realize it. There is only one potential problem, as I see it. If you are used to settling most issues mutually and are happy doing so, you may find that if you are faced with a difficult decision about which you strongly disagree, you will have a hard time handling it without it becoming a real source of trouble between you.

What happens is this: You, not realizing you have developed your own equalitarian ways, will still be giving verbal support to the hierarchical system in which the husband makes the final decisions. Since you so seldom are confronted with a major decision that you can't agree on, this final decision power is almost never exercised by the husband. But if a situation arises in which you need the negotiation skills of an equalitarian marriage whose participants have *decided* to operate in mutuality, but you do not have those skills because you have been thinking all along that you had a traditional marriage, you are bound to put a strain on your relationship.

The wife will find that she feels cheated and yet feels guilty because she feels this way. The husband will be forced to make a decision in a way he is not accustomed to and may feel unequal to. This becomes a wedge to drive the two of you apart.

If you go to your pastor for counsel in this case, he most probably will be a traditionalist, at least in theory, and will encourage the husband to decide and you to "submit." Neither of you is likely to be happy with this outcome, but you won't know just what went wrong. It would be much better if you would realize that you have a marriage based upon mutuality and go all the way with it, including major decisions.

My husband makes all the decisions and provides for all our needs. Both of us are very happy with this. I see no need for an equalitarian relationship. I feel happy and well-protected and my husband feels very important in my life.

If you are happy with this kind of marriage, I would not try to get you to change. But there are some considerations you may want to think about.

Is it fair to a man to make him solely responsible for your personal well-being? Many men carry extremely heavy loads trying to provide all the financial resources for the family and make all decisions too. It seems strange to insist that women need to be sheltered and protected from sharing the family responsibilities because they are more fragile and need a man to do it all when men frequently die before their wives. Maybe they aren't as strong and impervious to wear and tear as we would like to think. Maybe women *should* share more of the load than they do in such relationships.

Another factor you may want to consider is what might happen to you if you are widowed. We don't like to think of such a possibility, but it does happen.

A woman who has totally relied on her husband has often not learned self-reliance. Some widows find themselves in pitiful circumstances, having no idea how to manage their own finances and without any means to support themselves. This only adds to the emotional trauma of losing someone on whom you have been totally dependent.

It might be kinder to both you and your husband to have a more equal marriage.

My wife and I are so different that it seems impossible for us to work out any division of labor that would satisfy us both. We sometimes feel we don't even speak the same language. How can we ever have a marriage based upon mutual submission? We don't want the same things.

It probably won't be easy for you to get along no matter which kind of marriage you have. But I think you have more possibilities for making it in an equalitarian marriage than in the traditional kind because wide differences create an even greater need to find out what you both are really like. You need to learn to share and to know each other. Seeing each other as equals will help you accept your differences. Differences aren't bad in themselves. It's just that we often don't know what to do with them. Lasswell and Lobsenz in *No Fault Marriage* say:

> Most couples fail to realize that marital tensions do not arise so much out of the differences between partners as out of their inability to deal with them: to face them, express them openly, find ways to accept or bridge them. The point is not *whether* you and your husband or wife have divergent attitudes or disparate values. Of course you do. The point is whether you are able to explore, understand, and respect each other's value systems. Learning to be comfortable with the differences is a vital step in self-counseling.[1]

It is a mistake to assume that just because both of you are Christians your value systems will be the same and you will see things similarly.

Another writer talks about "scripts" that married partners have. He sees scripts as value systems based upon past experiences and associations.

For example, one man felt very strongly that sharing a double bed was important to a successful marriage. He voiced his preference for a double bed, but his wife, not knowing the script behind his choice, did not take him too seriously in the matter.

This husband and wife were at a furniture store looking for something one day when she saw twin beds on sale that she liked very much. She asked the salesperson to show them to her and expressed interest in buying them. Her husband became upset and embarrassed and insisted they leave. She was genuinely puzzled by his reaction. When he told her that he had been embarrassed because he felt her expressing a desire for twin beds to the salesperson gave the impression that their marriage was not doing so well, she knew she had to ask more.

He finally told her that his mother and father had enjoyed a good and happy marriage, and his mother had attributed part of its success to the fact that they always slept together in a large old double bed. When he had been about to marry, his mother had given him this advice: "Never get twin beds. That way you will never have the chance to go to bed angry with no way to make up. It's hard to stay mad when you are so close."

When this woman understood his value system in regard to beds, she was able both to reassure him that her interest in the beds had nothing to do with their marriage and to drop the idea of twin beds. She was more concerned about not threatening his feelings of security with her than in an attractive decorating idea.

If you regard your differences as areas you need to explore together instead of hurdles to jump over so you can both be on the same side of any issue, equal marriage can work well. If you have to force yourselves into traditional roles, though, you may find it is even harder to know each other and live in ways that are not a source for conflict.

I'm afraid my husband will feel less of a man if he has to give up his position of leader and decision maker and share it with me. I would like to work toward an equal relationship, but I don't want to threaten his masculinity or hurt him.

Many men have told me that they sometimes feel overwhelmed with all the pressures on them nowadays and would welcome some help in deciding and leading. This poem by Nancy R. Smith says it well.

> For every woman who is tired of acting weak when she
>   knows she is strong,
>   there is a man who is tired of appearing strong when he
>   feels vulnerable;
> For every woman who is tired of acting dumb,
>   there is a man who is burdened with the constant
>   expectation of "knowing everything";
> For every woman who is tired of being called
>   "an emotional female,"
>   there is a man who is denied the right to weep and to be
>   gentle;
> For every woman who is called unfeminine when she
>   competes,
>   there is a man for whom competition is the only way to
>   prove his masculinity;

> For every woman who is tired of being a sex object,
>   there is a man who must worry about his potency;
> For every woman who feels "tied down" by her children,
>   there is a man who is denied the full pleasure of shared
>   parenthood;
> For every woman who is denied meaningful employment
>   or equal pay
>   there is a man who must bear full financial responsibil-
>   ity for another human being;
> For every woman who was not taught the intricacies of an
>   automobile,
>   there is a man who was not taught the satisfactions of
>   cooking;
> For every woman who takes a step toward her own
>   liberation,
>   there is a man who finds the way to freedom has been
>   made a little easier.[2]

The *manner* of equalizing things in your relationship will probably make the difference. If you can share your feelings with you husband and tell him why you would like the change and that you are concerned about his own needs for self-confidence as a man and as a husband, you are likely to succeed much better than if you are either silent and do nothing or suddenly insist on changes at a time when you cannot share your whole concern in a kind and loving manner.

It is funny when you think of it—we say men are stronger than women, but we are afraid to approach them with new ideas because they might be more easily hurt than we are. I think men are stronger than that. If they are approached as people to share with, not someone to manipulate, they usually appreciate the consideration and react very well.

We like our work division the way it is. I want to stay home and care for my children and home. My husband wants to earn the living. Can we really have an equal marriage this way?

Yes, if this is the way you both decide you want to divide responsibilities. The important point is to make sure you both agree and that it is a fair distribution of labor and responsibilitiy. You should also be flexible enough to change any setup that gets to be uncomfortable for you if your needs or situations change.

There is nothing wrong with divisions of labor that follow traditional lines. The good thing about it is that you can cut up the work pie any way you want; you decide, not someone else.

You talk about "games" being destructive. I don't think I understand about these games. Could you explain further?

The term "games," as applied to secret interaction between people, comes from Transactional Analysis. TA, as it is often called, is a system for analyzing communication between people.

A communication exchange is called a "transaction." A transaction might involve any contact between two people whether verbal or not, but it is usually thought of in a verbal sense. A typical transaction might consist of my saying, "Hi, how are you?" You answer, "Fine." And I reply, "See you later." There isn't much in that transaction to analyze, but inflections in the voices or facial expressions could give the transaction extra meaning; then we could perhaps identify a game.

Games are a series of transactions that are used to get something in an undercover way, often without the participants realizing they are doing it for this purpose. It may be a means to control the other person, or even to get them to control us. These games are tools of manipulation.

Have you sometimes had the feeling when you've been with certain people that you've been "had" yet you don't know just how? Chances are you have had a game played on you.

Games are destructive to relationships because they block real communication and intimacy. They imply an unequal relationship. We use other people when we play these games.

If you observe yourself and your family for a few days, you may be able to spot recurring games you use on each other. You might even give them names, such as "How Could You Get Mad at a Poor Kid Like Me Who Can't Remember Anything," or, "Let's You and Him Fight."

There are several good books on Transactional Analysis that are helpful if you want to learn to identify and eventually stop playing games. *Born To Win* by Muriel James and Dorothy Jongeward is a good one to read if you're interested.

Speaking of books, can you recommend any that would be helpful to someone interested in equalizing their marriage?

There isn't much from the Christian perspective on equal marriage because the traditional hierarchical marriage has been considered to be the only permissible and biblical form for marriage for so long that Christian publishers have almost entirely limited themselves to books that support this view. The traditional interpretations of passages in the Bible concerning women's participation in the church and place in marriage have made this position nearly universal. There will undoubtedly be other books in the future, though, that will be both Christian in viewpoint and pro equality concerning marriage.

But for now, there are some secular books I can recommend to you for more information. *The Mirages of Marriage* by William J. Lederer and Don D. Jackson (Norton) has been out a few years, but it is still the best overall book on marriage that I know of. It is the kind of book you can read and then put down and have something to put into practice. So many books on marriage *sound* nice, but when you are through you wonder—what have I read that I can actually use?

Equal Marriage by Jean Stapleton and Richard Bright (Abingdon) is a small book with quite a few pointers on setting up an equal relationship.

The Kitchen Sink Papers by Mike McGrady (Doubleday) is both entertaining and informative. It is the account of a man's one-year stint as houseperson. Mike and Corinne McGrady traded places for one year so he could have "time off" and she could devote full-time attention to her growing plastics business. The book tells of Mike's education in the ways of housewifery with its joys and sorrows and charts the family's progress toward a mutual sharing of work and responsibility.

No-Fault Marriage by Marcia Lasswell and Norman M. Lobsenz (Doubleday) is a practical book of instruction on ways to help yourselves in marriage. They call their way "self-counseling." In the book they explain why you do some of the things you do in marriage that trip you up, and they tell how to go about changing things so you don't do them any more.

A little paperback called *Help Yourself* by John Lembo (Argus Publications) has information that can help you solve problems and generally get yourself together. Several of the Argus titles would be useful to couples working toward mutuality in marriage.

Husband and Wife by Peter DeJong and Donald R. Wilson (Zondervan) was written as a sociology textbook for Christian Colleges but is very worthwhile reading for those interested in biblical equal marriage.

Love and Negotiate by John Scanzoni (Word) is subtitled "Creative Conflict in Marriage." It's about how to negotiate and resolve conflicts in marriage through mutual submission. There are also chapters on negotiation in child rearing, in dating, and for single adults.

If both husband and wife share leadership, who will be the spiritual leader in the home?

I have always wondered why there needed to be only one person who leads the family in learning about and knowing God. Do we have to have a leader here? Can't we share this responsibility with even better results?

I have known many women who were concerned that their husbands learn to be spiritual leaders at home. These women were often well-versed in the Bible, knew enough to teach Sunday school classes, yet they felt they could not teach their own children because that was taking the husband's place. Women in this situation try all kinds of tactics to get the poor man to do his duty. They remind him (nag), try to butter him up by complimenting him on his spiritual growth (he knows it isn't true), and generally manage to kill any spark of initiative he had to begin with. And it isn't the women's fault.

It's the fault of the assumption that there has to be a spiritual leader at home and that this leader has to be male.

If the Holy Spirit gives you the ability and you gain the knowledge and the inclination to share with your family, it doesn't matter which gender you are. Share. If you can make learning about God and the Bible a pleasant experience your family wants to participate in, more power to you. And if you can work out some way of sharing it, that's even better. If not, then I say it doesn't matter. And I don't know of anything in the Bible that prevents you or even discourages you from it.

I want to have an equal marriage, but my wife/husband doesn't. What can I do?

First of all you should try to find out why they do not want to make a change. Is she afraid she will lose the security she now has as the one who is being taken care of? Or is he afraid he will lose his authority and control over you and the family? Do they think it is unbiblical? Are they afraid they will have to give up ways they know are wrong but which they want to keep anyway? If you can determine the reasons behind the resistance, then you can possibly think of ways to reduce it.

It is important to approach the subject in an non-judgmental manner. If you spring the idea on your spouse as a means to get them to shape up, you won't get far. And no one would blame them for resisting either.

Ask why they have aversion to looking into the subject. If they think it is unbiblical, perhaps they would be willing to study the subject with you if they think you are not out to overwhelm them with your own position. If equal marriage *is* biblical, it can stand close scrutiny by those who have doubts. That is not to say everyone will eventually be won over to equal marriage because of its utter reasonableness. But it helps to know that others who thought equal marriage was out of the question before they carefully examined the biblical evidence now are convinced it is biblical.

Maybe your spouse is stubborn and just doesn't like to change his/her mind. Give them time and room to make up their own mind in their own way. In the meantime, *you* can treat both of you as equal persons. You can consider yourself as someone who is of equal value so that you do not play underdog games or manipulate. You can treat your spouse as someone who is of equal value by giving the respect and consideration you would want if you were in their position. You can't guarantee that you will hit on what they really would want because that guessing game is never as good as being told, but your intention will shine through. And we can hope that eventually your actions will have an impact (like those of the women and men addressed in 1 Peter 3) on your husband's or wife's resistance and melt it away to the place where you can discuss the subject on a friendly and reasonable basis.

Won't all this throwing off of roles and stereotypes confuse children about which parent they are to model themselves after to have a healthy sexual identity? How will boys know what men are supposed to be like? How will girls know how to be feminine?

Down through history, and even today, men have done all kinds of work that women have done; yet we never seem to realize that a tailor's son does not feel like a woman because his father sews clothing for a living. He identifies with his father because: 1. He knows they are both male. 2. He has a good relationship with his father.

If a boy can identify in a positive way with a father who feels good about being a man, he will have no trouble accepting his maleness and seeing himself as male. But if his father is someone he does not want to be like, regardless of what he does in the way of being leader or follower or his occupation, he is more likely to have conflict about his sexual identity.

The same can be said for femininity. A girl wants to be like her mother when mother is a good woman to copy. It does not matter whether she is a truckdriver or a secretary. Sexual identity is with the person, not the occupation or share in leadership in the home.

Again, the relationship between family members seems to

be the most important factor in sexual identity, as it is in so many other areas.

My husband and I disagree about child rearing. How can we share this responsibility?

You ought to be able to work out at least a few general principles on raising children on which you can agree. That would help. But there is no reason why parents with different views can't share the care and guidance of their children.

You might tell them, if they are old enough, that you agree on some basics (if you do) but that you have different methods of dealing with them and different viewpoints.

One way to divide the discipline responsibility is to divide up the week between you. In some families mother has the job during the week and father has it on the weekend. All decisions except the really major ones (those you will have to work out together) are referred to the parent in charge. This way each parent gets a break, and they don't have to appear to agree all the time to present a united front.

But won't it confuse children to have two sets of rules, so to speak, to live by?

Not if the parents are reasonable people. Children always know you have different views on the subject anyway. One of childhood's favorite games is playing mom and dad against each other.

Sally goes to mom and says, "Mommy, can I go to Judy's and play?" Mommy says, "No, I don't think so—it's starting to rain. Better stay home."

Sally goes to dad. "Daddy," she says, sad-faced, "I want to go to Judy's and play." Daddy says, "That sounds like a good idea. Go ahead."

Sally returns to mom. "Mommy, daddy says I can go."

Sound familiar?

If the parents have split up the responsibility, mom or dad (whoever is off that day) can say, "Go ask your father/mother. He/she is the decider today."

Now, at first Sally will say, "But mommy, he might say no. He isn't as kind as you are," or something else designed to get sympathy. Mom replies, "That's too bad—maybe you can ask again when it's my turn."

Children know we aren't the same. They learn quickly.

---

1. Lasswell and Lobsenz, *No-Fault Marriage,* p. 88.

2. Nancy R. Smith, "For Every Woman," *Images: Women in Transition* (Nashville: The Upper Room, 1976), p. 52.

HEIRS
TOGETHER

13

13

Gestalt

We've walked through new territory in this book, gently and considerately I hope. I want to finish this walk together with a sense of completeness. Not that I expect to have said the last word on the subject or presented the total picture of what equal marriage is like or how to go about it. No, I hope this will be only a beginning of thinking and writing about biblically equalitarian marriage.

What I want to do is look back over the book and see it as a whole. Also, I think we should consider the subject of completeness itself as it relates to marriage.

Marriage Is a Relationship

We looked at marriage historically and sociologically and discovered that there are many different types of marriage and different ways of living within marriage. The relationship between the two partners seemed to be the only element of marriage that is common to all. Because of this, the relationship itself became the focus of our study. The state of the relationship within marriage makes it either satisfying or uncomfortable for its partners. Fortunately, the relationship is the one part of marriage that anyone can work on regardless of social situations or marriage customs and laws.

Biblical Guidelines for Relationships

The principle of mutual submission as presented in Ephesians 5:21 shines out as the overriding principle for relationships in the church, the home, and at work. This "I am as valuable as you are and you are as valuable as I am" principle can be used by believers, with the Holy Spirit's guidance, to achieve unity in the church, harmony and growth in the home, and to express the love we have for one another. It is a means to avoid wasting any of God's gifts to us.

For working out the details, we have our own good common sense, the experiences of others shared with us, and God's guidance from within.

Completeness

We, as Christians, believe that God fulfills us, adds that something we were missing before Christ came into our lives. We see Jesus as the fullness of God's love and provision for our needs. We talk about maturing in Christ and growing up to our full size spiritually. Yet when we come to marriage, we do a surprising turnaround. We, as Christians, also share a common belief that we are not quite whole people until we are married.

The opinion that one must be married to be whole, revealed only half-jokingly in talk about "my better half," has some unfortunate results. It causes unmarried Christians who are beyond the customary age for marriage to be regarded as less than whole people. Unmarried people are often subtly given the message that something must be wrong with them.

But is this true? Does marriage, union with another person in matrimony, take two partial people and make one whole entity? We talk about becoming "one," as though separately we are not already each *one* to begin with.

Perhaps we are confusing two meanings of the concept of

unity. Unity can mean different incomplete elements converging to create a complete unit. Or, unity can mean whole and complete-in-themselves units banding together for a common goal. In the former case, many parts make one whole. In the latter, many wholes make a unified effort, a unified cooperation. I believe that the biblical instructions about mutual submission and the unity of believers is talking about the second kind of unity—that of whole people cooperating. Christ has already made each one whole; now they are uniting for common purposes. In biblical marriage, the same kind of unity is called for. It takes two whole people to have a *whole* marriage.

It is not hard to find the origin of the idea that marriage partners are not complete people separately. Medieval theologians did not believe women were whole persons. As they put it, the woman alone was not in the image of God, but could be when joined to her husband. English common law did not regard a wife as a whole person but as a part of her husband.

Also, in the past the need for a male heir to pass one's property on to probably made most men feel incomplete until they had acquired a wife to provide that son. The business of growing up and becoming a mature man would have been incomplete without a wife to provide descendants.

The tragedy is that this belief that marriage partners are incomplete before marriage has had a harmful effect upon marriage. If two people approach marriage feeling that it will make them complete, they are automatically setting themselves up for a disillusioning experience. Immaturity does not disappear with the signing of a marriage license. Emotional hang-ups do not fall away just because you have wed. You will still be you.

This belief that marriage completes us and thus somehow solves our problems contributes to disappointment with marriage. After the beautiful ceremony is over and fairy-tale clothes are put away, everything else can seem downhill if magical solutions to feelings of inadequacy were expected.

But if two whole people come together as a *team*, a satisfying and realistic relationship can be built.

Gestalt

I do like the German word *gestalt*. My fourth-year-German-student son, David, explained it to me once, and it has been a favorite of mine ever since. Like many other good words it has rich shades of meaning and is difficult to translate precisely. *Gestalt* describes the feeling that everything fits together and has been brought to a satisfying completion. It is like a closed circle. No loose ends. It doesn't mean the end of a good thing, but that everything has worked out well.

I would like to leave you with *gestalt*.

I've shared my own personal journey toward equal marriage and what I have learned about it. I have looked at it biblically, historically, and practically. I feel good about equal marriage because it *is* biblical and practical. Sometimes Christians are hesitant to say something is reasonable or practical as an indication that it is right because they don't want to appear to be adapting their faith to what is merely convenient. And it is good to be aware of that possibility. But I have noticed that what God teaches us is ultimately the most practical way to do anything. He is the supreme realist.

So, I hope this book provides some *gestalt* for you in the presentation of information and ideas that you can use. But most of all, I hope that you two can create your own *gestalt* together, beginning now.

Subject
Index

Scripture
Index

Subject Index

Scripture Index